A Portrait of Leadership
A Fighter for Health

THE HONORABLE

PAUL GRANT ROGERS

The new kid on the block, 1955. Paul Rogers' official congressional photo.

A Portrait of Leadership
A Fighter for Health

THE HONORABLE

PAUL GRANT ROGERS

Roger J. Bulger, MD

Shirley Sirota Rosenberg

with

Bob Maher • Steve Lawton • Jeff Schwartz

Printed in the United States of America

ISBN 1-891524-11-9

The Association of Academic Health Centers (AHC) is a national, nonprofit organization dedicated to improving the health of the people by advancing the leadership of academic health centers in health professions education, biomedical and public health research, and health care delivery.

The views expressed in this book are those of the authors and do not necessarily represent the views of Carden Jennings Publishing Co., Ltd., the Board of Directors of the Association of Academic Health Centers or the AHC membership at large.

Library of Congress Cataloging-in-Publication Data

A Portrait of leadership, a fighter for health : the Honorable Paul Grant Rogers / by Roger J. Bulger ... [et al].
p. cm.
ISBN 1-891524-11-9
1. Rogers, Paul G. 2. Health services administrators – United States – Biography. 3. Legislators – United States – Biography. 4. Health lawyers – United States – Biography. 5. Public health laws – United States – History – 20th century. 6. Environmental policy – United States – History – 20th century. 7. Medical policy – United States – History – 20th century. I. Bulger, Roger J., 1933- II. Title.

RA424.5.R58P55 2005
362.1'092–dc22 2005000242

To all those who work to promote health, cure disease, and improve the health status of the entire population while bringing hope and succor to those still suffering.

Contents

Foreword

As a relatively young physician, I attended an event in Aspen, Colorado, in the summer of 1975 where the featured speaker was Congressman Paul Rogers. Hearing him in person for the first time, I was struck by his mastery of the material and his cogent arguments. Especially impressive were his responses to challenging questions. He marshaled facts and apt illustrations as if he had been expecting exactly the question asked. Persuasive without being argumentative, he made it easy to agree with him. In a few minutes, anyone present could see why Paul Rogers was such a successful legislator.

In this book, the authors tell the story of Paul Rogers' achievements in the Congress and beyond. It is not merely the tale of a triumphant legislator who justly earned the appellation Mr. Health. Rather, it is an unfinished play in two acts covering 24 years in the Congress and 24 more in the private sector. For nearly a half-century, Paul Rogers has crafted and influenced policy that has improved the health and quality of life of every person in the United States. The quality of air we breathe, the clean water we drink, the protection of the public's health, the provision of basic medical services, and the scientific research that makes progress possible all today bear the imprint of Paul Rogers.

This record of accomplishment is remarkable for its range, depth, and duration. The reader will see how skillfully Paul Rogers amplified and capitalized on any post he held. But his success transcends the power inherent in any particular position. In both the private and public sectors, Paul Rogers has been the author of his own achievement, and the pages that follow capture the qualities of leadership that Paul Rogers exemplifies.

His legacy will endure, and those of us who have been privileged to know, interact, and benefit from him will be forever grateful to him and for him. Paul Rogers remains a vital force for promoting science, advancing health, and improving the environment, and his is a life worth knowing and emulating. This book helps us to do both.

Harvey V. Fineberg
President
Institute of Medicine

Preface

This is a book about Paul Grant Rogers, a man who has dedicated almost five decades of his professional life to improving the well-being of all Americans. He spent 24 years (1956–1979) in the United States Congress where he authored an astounding variety of health and environmental legislation, retiring from the House of Representatives with the title Mr. Health. From 1980 to the present, as a partner and member of the Health Section of the Hogan & Hartson law firm in Washington, D.C., his dedication to health has been expressed in an astonishingly wide variety of mostly pro bono activities. And although Paul Rogers has never personally managed more than his own staff, his business has always been one of grand proportions, where he has consistently served as chairman of the board.

Paul Rogers, indisputably the nation's leader in the field of health, has changed the landscape of American healthcare, whether with carefully paced steps or in one grand sweep. Along the way, he has attracted followers, including former naysayers, to his causes. But *A Portrait of Leadership, A Fighter for Health: The Honorable Paul Grant Rogers* is more than a chronology of his remarkable achievements on Capitol Hill and elsewhere. It is also the story of a leader who continues, even as a private citizen, to extend his reach beyond his immediate domain into the realm of public policy and thereby to affect entire sectors of society.

Thus, in addition to being a book about a great American, this work is also about leadership. We trust that his story will resonate with those people who face what may be perhaps the most demanding leadership challenge of all: the management of academic health centers and their teaching hospitals within an academic setting. We also hope it will prove to be worthy of extension to other fields as well.

The major sources for this book are fourfold: (1) historical fact, of course; (2) the writings of grand thinkers and practitioners in the field of organizations, leadership, and human behavior; (3) the recollections of friends and of colleagues who have witnessed how Rogers goes about his business, including his work as counsel to the Association of Academic Health Centers; and (4) hours upon hours of conversation separately spent by the authors with Becky and Paul Rogers.

The introduction describes the temper of the times into which Paul Rogers was born. In chapters 1 through 4, we follow Rogers into the House of Representatives, where he was a fledgling congressman from Florida at first concerned only about his immediate constituents, and watch him evolve into a champion of the best possible health for all Americans. Rogers' reentry into private life, to which he brings the political acumen, forceful personality, leadership prowess, and network of health advocates developed as a congressman, makes up chapters 5 through 9.

Chapter 10 sets the stage for a comparison of Paul Rogers as a leader with the leadership qualities espoused by such organizational thinkers as James McGregor Burns, Daniel Goleman, Jim Collins, and John Gardner. The writings on human behavior by physicians Victor Frankl, William Osler, George Engel, and Leston Havens, as well as nurse Florence Nightingale, also inform the authors' view of how Rogers' professional life mirrors the best in leadership.

All of this leads to chapter 11, which sets forth the Rogers Model—an example of leadership whose defining characteristics are prudence and wisdom based on core values, an awareness of societal and public policy, and a sensitivity that transcends one's own self-interest to embrace the public interest or the interests of those the organization serves.

Chapter 12 contains a dialogue between Roger Bulger and Paul Rogers in which the nation's Mr. Health presents his current thinking and recommendations concerning the future of health, health-related policy, and biomedical research in America.

In recent decades, many scholars have pointed out that the observer, the social scientist, and even the so-called hard scientist influence the outcome of their work through their biases and beliefs, no matter how hard they try to be totally objective. It is, therefore, incumbent upon authors to speak to their readers about the personal perspectives they bring to their writings, especially those opinions that, consciously or subconsciously, may have influenced their selection of materials, observations, and conclusions.

One personal bias derives from Bulger's belief that leadership in the healthcare field has great healing dimensions of its own; a second bias is that good leadership can be learned through emulation, study, and experience. Bulger also holds that whether by birth or design, the best leadership is present in certain outstanding individuals who have a vision and mission that are supra-personal, allowing them to carry along others who share the vision, adopt it with enthusiasm, and even go on to become leaders themselves. Paul Rogers is such a man.

Acknowledgments

We must first thank the John J. McGovern Foundation for its three-year grant to the Association of Academic Health Centers for work exploring ethics and human values in healthcare, including the scholarly effort that went into the analysis of the leadership literature at the heart of this book. Most of the last grant year has been spent exploring these issues in the context of the medical and healthcare professions. Without the foundation's support, this project could never have succeeded. In addition, for more than three decades, Dr. McGovern has personally provided the lead author, Roger J. Bulger, with sage advice and encouragement to keep the themes of human values and ethics before the clinician community. He has also provided many different grants to facilitate such work in healthcare and academic healthcare institutions. We are grateful for this help, too.

We also express our gratitude to Anne S. Wood, an associate editor at SSR, Incorporated, whose creative spirit and steady hand at every stage of this work helped us see this book to press.

The authors thank the Association of Academic Health Centers for supporting this book project over the past year and hope that the product will be shown to merit their investment. We also thank both Research!America, especially Mary Woolley, and Hogan & Hartson LLP, especially Ann Vickery, for their substantive support and input. JoAnne Glisson's sharp eye, combined with her experience as a professional staffer for Congressman Rogers, helped put the final touches on the manuscript.

Both Paul and Becky Rogers have been open, resourceful, and patient in helping us find source documents, letters, and photographs, not to mention making themselves available for interviews and to answer questions. From this experience, we understand why so many of their friends were also generous with their time and input. Among them are John Whitehead, John Seffrin, Senator Arlen Spector, The Honorable Robert Michel, The Honorable John Porter, Senator Tom Harkin, Dr. William Peck, and Governor Robert Ray. Also, Stuart Ross, Bette Ann Starkey, Robert Lochrie, Cass Wheeler, The Honorable Dan Mica, Judith Cranford, and Sandra Raymond. Our thanks to all.

Our sincerest appreciation is due to the indefatigable Ken Massey and Debbie Bretches of Carden Jennings Publishing Co., Ltd., who guided this book handily through the many twists and turns it took on the way to press.

A Note From Roger Bulger:

As a personal friend and professional colleague of Paul Rogers since 1988, I felt fairly confident as I started this book that I could write about the post-congressional period of his life. However, after meeting with Mr. Rogers' congressional staff as a group and then individually, I realized that, in view of their enthusiasm for the project and the wealth of material that came out at what turned out to be their first reunion in some time, I wasn't the best person to write about his congressional years. Heaven sent, as far as this project was concerned, was Bob Maher, a journalist and writer by trade who worked closely with Congressman Rogers for many years. Maher's exquisite storytelling was amplified by the reminiscences of two colleagues from those legislative years, former chief counsel Steve Lawton and professional staffer Jeff Schwartz. Together, they have brought Rogers' legislative years to life in an extraordinarily compelling way.

As I talked with more and more of Mr. Rogers' colleagues and friends, as well as a broad range of political observers and experts, it became clear to me that our subject was a leader of extraordinary dimensions and that it was incumbent on me to weave the complexities of leadership into the health-policy fabric that Mr. Rogers has been consistently producing for close to a half-century.

Naturally, such a complex effort would require a terrific editor-writer, and we at the Association of Academic Health Centers knew such a person very well. Shirley Sirota Rosenberg has worked on a variety of publications with members of our staff, including myself, and came on board to put the story together, help us speak in a consistent voice, keep us objective and organized, and see the book to press. Shirley also realized that there must have been something about the years before Paul Rogers became Mr. Health that were important to the ultimate goals of this book. So she developed the introduction, thereby laying the base for the story. She joins me as coauthor of *A Portrait of Leadership, A Fighter for Health: The Honorable Paul Grant Rogers.*

Paul, about 6 years old. There was always a pet in the Rogers' house, but in the '20s, the Rin Tin Tin movie character made the German Shepherd one of the most coveted by children.

Introduction

The Early Years

On January 11, 1955, Paul Grant Rogers was sworn in as the representative of Florida's Sixth Congressional District. He was 34 years old, a conservative Democrat from a conservative district in a conservative state, filling the post of his late father, Dwight Laing Rogers Sr. Sam Rayburn, the legendary Speaker of the House from Texas, administered the oath. Eisenhower was President. Elected to Congress 12 times in all, Paul Rogers served under five more Presidents: Kennedy, Johnson, Nixon, Ford, and Carter.

Paul Rogers was born on June 4, 1921, in the tiny town of Ocilla in south-central Georgia, where his father, Dwight Sr., practiced law and his mother, Florence Roberts Rogers, tended home. When he was four, the family, which included an older son, Dwight Jr., moved to south Florida where the third son, Doyle, was born. The Rogers first lived in Delray (now Delray Beach) and then moved on to Ft. Lauderdale. With about 6,500 residents, Ft. Lauderdale was double the size of Ocilla.

In 1920, Florida, two-thirds rural, had an economy largely derived from winter vegetables. With a population of 968,470*, Florida was the

---

* According to the 1920s terminology of the U.S. Census Bureau, Florida's population

least-populated state on the southeast coast.[1] Agricultural acreage was expanding with inexpensive crops like lettuce, green beans, and corn in South Florida, now growing in the newly drained swamplands around Lake Okeechobee (Big Water). The soil around the lake was so rich in organic matter it would spontaneously combust during a protracted heat wave. From an airplane, it looked as though a giant black magic marker had cut a wide swath through the land. North Florida grew pecans and some tobacco. Everywhere, migrant workers tilled the soil.

The early 1920s were heady years for Florida. Wealthy people were flocking to Palm Beach, a spit of land fronting the Atlantic Ocean, building lavish estates and bringing in world-renowned celebrities to entertain and mix with the guests. The Intercoastal Waterway, along with Lake Worth, separated Palm Beach from West Palm Beach, where the Palm Beach staff and other workers lived.

The boom times also brought to Florida middle-class families lured by sand, sea, and opportunity. With the end of World War I, incomes were generally on the rise; salaried employees were beginning to receive some work benefits, including vacation time; and automobile prices were coming down. Tourists, even from abroad, were flocking to the Sunshine State. To attract yet more tourists, the state launched a program of rail and road construction, supplementing the private rail lines (the Flagler line along the east coast and the Plant line across the midlands and along the western coast) that were already opening the southern part of the peninsula to trade as well as to the resorts . The citrus industry now started to grow. (Florida today is the nation's premier citrus producer.) Land investors and speculators were not far behind, and credit was easy to obtain.

The Rogers family arrived just in time for the bust. By 1926, the credit and money had run out. Hurricanes over the next two years wrought more havoc, bringing on floods in the Everglades that decimated the crops and took the lives of 2,000 people. In 1929, the Mediterranean fruit fly cut

---

comprised 532,295 Native Whites of native parentage; 62,850 Native Whites of foreign or mixed parentage; 43,008 Foreign-Born Whites; 329,487 Negroes; 518 Indians; 181 Chinese; 106 Japanese; and 25 Other. In 1921, most American Indians were living on reservations established during the early 20th century. In Florida, most of their forebears, primarily Seminole, had been relocated to Oklahoma by the mid-1800s.

citrus production by about 60 percent. The Great Depression had come early to Florida. It was not until the advent of World War II that the state would start to fully recover.

Although Dwight Sr. had invested in an orange grove in Winter Haven in central Florida even before he came to Florida, his family neither profited nor suffered substantially from the boom-and-bust days. They remained a resolutely middle-class family, Paul Rogers recalls, and always seemed "to be able to manage without difficulty."

It was assumed in the Rogers family that the three sons would follow their father into law, and indeed all eventually did. But theirs was not only a lawyerly family. It was a political family, too. In addition to handling his law practice, Dwight Sr. served in the state legislature between 1930 and 1938, rising to the post of Speaker pro tem in 1933.* So even before their father went on to the U.S. Congress, the three brothers were introduced to the ways of politics.

Paul Rogers attended the public schools of Broward County. By the time he graduated from the city's only public high school in 1938, Ft. Lauderdale's population had swollen to 18,000. Yet it was decades away from being the major tourist capital for Middle America. Orange and grapefruit groves flourished near the city limits, and a small farm community at the city's southern end proclaimed itself the Tomato Capital of the World.

Matriculating at the University of Florida, Rogers studied political science with a minor in speech. He got involved with the debating team, winning the international award from the Tau Kappa Alpha Debating Society after a bout with Oxford University, and campus politics, helping to put a few classmates into office. He joined the ROTC (Reserve Officers Training Corps) and upon graduation in June 1942, he was called into service as an Army second lieutenant.

The tour of duty broadened the world for the country boy from Florida. "Most important," he says, "I saw how much, working together, people could accomplish to reach a goal. And I brought that back with me to civilian life." After two years of training in the states, he was detailed to

---

* One of his many accomplishments is the Florida Homestead Act of 1935, wherein the owner of a property legally declared a homestead receives certain protections from creditors and a $5,000 tax exemption on the assessed value ($25,000 now).

Europe, primarily the northeastern sector, as a field artillery planning and fire control officer. He participated in the Battle of the Pocket in December 1944. In late March 1945, he was in the final assault on Germany, the Battle of the Rhine, during which the combined American, British, and Canadian forces crossed the last natural border between the Allies and the Axis Powers. He came home a year later with the Bronze Star medal with two battle stars and the rank of major.

Back in the states, Paul went on to law school. He spent the first semester at George Washington University in Washington, D.C., where, with Dwight Sr.'s election to Congress, the family had established a second residence. Paul Rogers knew, however, that if he wanted to practice law back home or become involved in state politics, it was better to have a degree from Florida's leading law school. He transferred to the University of Florida, earning his law degree in 1948.

To avoid making his father's firm Rogers-top-heavy (his brother Dwight was already a partner), Paul decided to practice law in West Palm Beach in Palm Beach County, settling in with the law firm Alley, Drew, Burns, and Middleton. The city, once primarily an adjunct to nearby Palm Beach, was now thriving on its own. (Brother Doyle also chose Palm Beach County for his law practice.) Within a few years, Paul Rogers was made a name partner. However, his legal career went on hold when his father, at age 68, died of a heart attack in December 1954, a month after reelection to his sixth congressional term without opposition. The governor of Florida called a special election to fill the seat.*

The Rogers name would give a Rogers a good shot at the father's seat. Dwight Jr. was the logical choice, but at 38 years of age, he was married, raising a family, and running a successful practice at his father's law firm. He had no interest in running for office. Doyle, at 27, was not yet professionally established, having gone into Army service after undergraduate college. Paul, a bachelor, stepped forward. He enjoyed public speaking and was the son most attracted to politics. With brother Dwight helping run his campaign,

* Unlike the U.S. Senate, where a vacant seat is filled by the governor's appointee, all vacancies in the House—i.e., the people's house—during the first session of a Congress must be filled by a special election in the district as required by the Constitution.

Paul Rogers garnered 68 percent of the House votes in a five-candidate field. So he boarded a plane and flew to Washington.

His district extended across the entire width of Florida's midsection—from the east to the west coast. Newcomers to Florida typically populated one coast or the other; those from the Midwest dominated the west coast and those from the Northeast dominated the east coast. Both coasts housed a predominantly white population. Inland between was working-class Florida, primarily agricultural, with a large black population from the Deep South and the Caribbean Islands.

At the time Paul Rogers was born, healthcare was available only from private practitioners, usually the family doctor. Very few employers provided healthcare benefits, and fraternal and benevolent organizations took up some of the slack, but paying medical bills was a big stretch for most Americans. Hospitals were concentrated in the big cities (and were not necessarily to be trusted), and most people in small towns were born, cared for, and died at home.

Although the health of Americans had been consistently improving over the years, life expectancy in 1920 was only 53.6 years for men and 54.6 for women.[2] Out of every 1,000 deliveries, 8 resulted in the death of the mother.[3] Orphaned children were not uncommon, and Little Orphan Annie easily struck a sympathetic chord when her cartoon strip debuted in 1925. Childhood diseases were taking lives too, with an infant mortality rate of 85 out of every 1,000 live births annually.[4] Other children were left with chronic problems.

By the time Rogers assumed his congressional seat, the impact of medical discoveries (penicillin itself was a revolution); public health campaigns; and concerted environmental, public health, social welfare, clinical medicine, and hospital-based interventions were being felt throughout the land.

During the war, the Roosevelt Administration and the labor unions had reached an agreement: With salaries frozen, employers were permitted to give health benefits to employees in lieu of pay raises. The wartime stratagem served as the model for health-benefit plans fast becoming a fixture in many industries. Access to low-cost or free healthcare was also improving, primarily through clinics set up by the U.S. Public Health Service and under U.S. Children's Bureau grants to the states.

As a result, life expectancy for men rose to 65.6 years by 1950. For women, it was now up to 71.1 years,[5] a reflection in part of the dramatic decrease in maternal deaths from childbirth (to 0.83 out of 1,000).[6] Infant mortality, in turn, sank to 29.2 per 1,000 live births a year.[7]

In Florida, now the fastest growing state in the nation, another economic boom was underway, and an urban society was beginning to emerge. Despite all the good news, significant disparities in health status persisted, both in the state and across the nation.

He didn't know it then, but the new Congressman Rogers had more work cut out for him than he could ever have imagined.

PART I

The Legislative Years

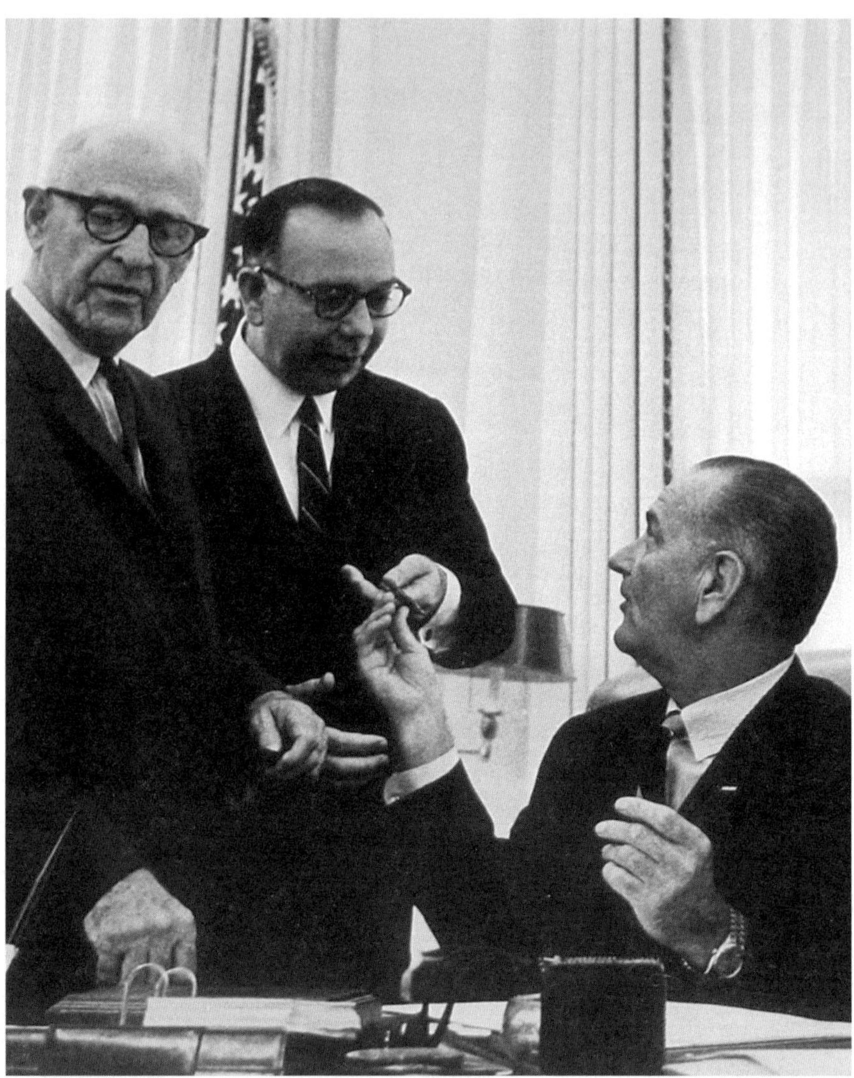

A White House ceremony, October 22, 1965. Lyndon Johnson presents Rogers with one of the pens he used to sign H.R. 3141. The legislation was for improving the quality of medical education, extending loans and scholarships to medical students, and constructing new health-professions educational facilities. To the left is co-sponsor Senator Lister Hill (D-Ala.).

Chapter 1

Paul Rogers, Congressman from Florida

Paul Rogers was sworn in only five days after the other members of the congressional class of January 1955. Assigned to his father's office in the Longworth Building, he inherited and kept his father's staff, but he could not get his father's assignment to the House Health and Safety Committee. Instead, his first major committee was the Committee on Public Works; his minor committee was the Merchant Marine and Fisheries Committee. He had miles to go before he would acquaint himself with issues of health, environment, and the host of alphabet agencies he would eventually come to oversee and guide.

Certainly, those in the nation's capital who met Paul Rogers in professional and social settings would have had trouble detecting any sign of a small-town boy in the new congressman. Impeccably dressed, shoes shined to mirror finish, a tasteful tie topping off his trademark high collar, Rogers was the epitome of sophistication. He was also truly charming.

As each census reflected the exuberant growth of Florida's population, Rogers' district was divided and renumbered accordingly. During his last few terms, he had the largest congressional district in the nation. Spread over 12 counties with a population nearing 900,000, it was larger than some states. But even though Florida was growing more urban than rural, Rogers' district remained primarily agricultural. Winter crops were still a

LIKE FATHER, LIKE SON

Driving with staffer Bob Maher through Immokalee, a small Florida farming town, Rogers remembered how he'd go there to campaign with his father when his father was running for re-election.

"We were walking down the street one day and, of course, we were running a little late, when Dad saw this man out on a dock. Suddenly, he took off for the dock, where he talked to this man for a while. I was a little antsy. We were late, and he was taking time to go out there to see that guy. I figured that man must be important or maybe a good friend, so, when he returned, I asked my dad, 'Do you know that guy? Is he a friend?' He answered, 'No. But my dad taught me that if you treat a man like a friend, he'll be your friend.'"

mainstay of Florida's economy, although sugar had become king. The southernmost rim of Lake Okeechobee was now the southern boundary of the sugar lands that were producing most of the nation's cane sugar. The industry grew especially rapidly when imports from Cuba were banned after the Cuban revolution and Cuban refugees, with their sugar-growing skills, arrived in Florida.

In a district with such a widely dispersed population, Rogers frequently took to the road to meet with fellow Floridians. He was as comfortable talking to the woman who ran the local store as he was chatting at a charity event in Palm Beach. Despite the heat, Rogers always wore his standard blue suit, white shirt, and tie when he was visiting the people in his district. Both he, and his father before him, felt that constituents expected it of their congressman. When he ran for office, he ran hard. And he ran hard in Washington as well.

One of the best ways to get around the sprawling Capitol compound is via the underground tunnel system that links the House and Senate office buildings and the Capitol. A subway (actually, an open tram with a few connecting cars) also connects some of these buildings, but many people on the Hill prefer to hoof it instead.

Paul Rogers was doing just that one day when he noticed a beautiful woman walking the other way. He was so struck by her that he immediately checked to find out who she was and where she worked, along with her telephone number. She was Rebecca (Becky) Bell Mosely, a young widow and

Capitol Hill staffer, who had also come to the Hill at the same time as Rogers. She was also from the South, had grown up in a small town, and was a Democrat, to boot. Rebecca had come to Washington to join the staff of Congressman George Grant (D-Ala.), where she handled constituent correspondence and casework on behalf of constituents in need of help.

Becky was one of four daughters and a son born to Joseph Vernon Bell, a successful local businessman, and his wife Nell, in Andalusia, Alabama, a town of 10,000.* "I was very happy in that world," she recalls. In late 1954, on a visit home, Congressman Grant had been quietly looking around for someone suitable to work in his Washington office. When he learned that Becky might be available, he came to talk with her at her home. He quickly became convinced that, even without political experience, she would soon master the skills he needed for the Washington office. She accepted his job offer, and began work just as the new congressional session was about to start, moving into an apartment in Georgetown that she shared with other young women working on Capitol Hill. She adjusted quickly to her job, made many new friends, and enjoyed Washington's unique social scene.

A mutual friend, Newton Steers, an investor who later became a Republican congressman from Maryland, was eventually to become the matchmaker. Paul and he had been part of the eligible-bachelor set in Washington, and Paul was a groomsman at his wedding to Nina Auchinchloss, stepsister to Jackie Kennedy. Newton introduced Becky and Paul.

Becky and Paul dated for about a year, their free time frequently dictated by what was happening on the Hill or even in the world. As a result, Paul's mother didn't meet Becky until they were engaged to each other and only a few weeks away from their wedding ceremony at her parents' house on December 15, 1962.

After the wedding, Paul left his quarters at the Wardman Park, where he had lived for a half-dozen years, Becky left her apartment-share, and the two moved into an apartment in northwest Washington, D.C.

---

* Originally settled by the Creek Indians, the town's name means "to walk" (ande) and "easy" (lutier) in Spanish. It presumably derives from the Spaniards who explored the area in the late 15th century.

Throughout his congressional career, and for many years afterward, they also maintained a residence in West Palm Beach.

The Rogers moved twice more, each time into a house of their own in Washington's Spring Valley neighborhood. However, says Paul Rogers, if he had his way, they would live in a hotel like he once did. "Just think of all the chores you don't have to do," he reminisces.

Rebecca Laing Rogers was born on October 8, 1963. She bears her grandfather's middle name and is popularly known as Laing. After attending the National Cathedral School for Girls in Washington, she matriculated at Duke University and started on a possible career in the New York City fashion business, working and even modeling for such big-name designers as Calvin Klein and Adrienne Vittadini.

Laing married John Michael Sisto in May 1987. They have three daughters and a son. "I guess she didn't like being an only child," Becky laughs. The Sistos live in Westfield, New Jersey. Laing is a homemaker and also active in community affairs, particularly health concerns, and John is a successful building and demolition contractor. The two families are very close.

For most of his time on the Hill, Rogers read every piece of mail coming into and going out of his office and personally signed every letter that bore his signature. Each year, too, Rogers sent out a short questionnaire (it fit on a postcard) so he could better gauge constituent concerns. The completed cards were returned promptly in record numbers. People liked to have their congressman asking their opinion on specific issues. By coincidence, just as his involvement in shaping health legislation increased, the proportion of elderly people in his district grew dramatically, many of them having relocated from the Northeast to the sunny retirement communities of Florida. The letters came in, hundreds a week. If a constituent had a problem with Social Security, Rogers would send a letter letting her know that he was contacting the Social Security Administration on her behalf. Many letters from the elderly demanded legislation that would result in a government-run healthcare system, a concept that Rogers was never comfortable with, although he later came to consider the concept of universal healthcare coverage financed by a private-government partnership as a viable option.

Rogers' hallmark was returning leftover campaign money to his contributors based on the percentage of unspent contributions. Many checks ran to only two or three dollars, and it was not unusual for constituents to pull a check out of their wallet and proudly display it, uncashed, many years later.

The Republicans in Palm Beach readily forgave him his political party and enthusiastically supported him in elections. When George McGovern, running for the Presidency against Richard Nixon in 1972, captured only a quarter of the vote in Rogers' district, Rogers himself won handily.

When he first came into Congress, the needs of his state, and particularly, his district, were uppermost in Rogers' mind. Thus, his Migrant Health Act, 1962, provided healthcare to a population with few resources and no fixed addresses. As a member of the Merchant Marine and Fisheries Committee, he wrote a report on the potential of marine resources to the nation. After visiting Russia on behalf of the committee, he told the nation, "Every other fish in the American frying pan was landed by Russian fishermen." Despite his junior standing, he went on to spend a considerable amount of time helping develop the House version of the Senate-inspired Sea Grant College Act of 1966 and guiding it through the House.

The act was to do the same for farming the seas as the Land Grant College Act had done for farming the land. At the time, some interesting studies were pointing to the possibility of mining the seas for minerals and pharmaceutical products, as well as food. The oceans were our last unexplored and undeveloped frontier. Pure research into new products from the sea seemed to be a good investment for the nation as well as a possible boon to Florida's relatively large marine industry. Rogers also realized that at least two universities in Florida had fledgling programs that could be built up with such help.

Rogers' work on the bill led to his appointment to the National Commission on the Oceans. The group included experts on all aspects of the seas and produced the most definitive report ever written on the domain that covers three-quarters of Earth. Many of the responsibilities of the National Oceanic and Atmospheric Administration, established in 1970, were originally set forth in the report.

One day, as Rogers was preparing his materials for a conference with the Senate on reconciling the differences in their versions of the Sea Grant College bill, fledgling staffer Bob Maher asked if he could come along. At the time, it was an unwritten rule that only the counsel from the full committee working on the bill attended such conferences. Rogers outlined the conditions: if anyone said anything, Maher would have to leave.

Rogers entered the conference room, staffer in tow, to be greeted by other House members. He then went around the room greeting his Senate counterparts, pulling Maher along and introducing him to each senator, in turn: Jacob Javits, Warren Magnuson, Claiborne Pell, and a young Ted Kennedy, an impressive array of Senate luminaries.

The bell rang, calling the House members to a vote. As Rogers and Maher walked through the Capitol tunnel to the House side, a stocky man in a black suit strode purposely toward Rogers, smiling beneath rimless glasses, hand extended. It was Supreme Court Justice Byron (Whizzer) White.

"What are *you* doing here?" Rogers asked in mock amazement and then turned to his assistant. "Mr. Justice, this is Bob Maher. He works with me."

Maher never forgot the thrill of meeting all those senators, let alone Justice White. It did, however, take a long time for him to fully comprehend that no one ever worked *for* Paul Rogers. His staff all worked *with* him.

PUBLIC HEALTH AND WELFARE SUBCOMMITTEE

Rogers was appointed to his father's committee in 1961, now called the Public Health and Welfare Subcommittee. The chairman, Kenneth Roberts (D-Ala.), was subsequently followed in the mid '60s by John Jarman (D-Okla.), a dapper dresser with a perennial tan. Jarman's interest ran more toward transportation and energy issues important to his state. Rogers' willingness to organize and conduct the health subcommittee hearings lightened Jarman's schedule, and he granted Rogers much latitude. In effect, Rogers ran the health subcommittee for half-a-dozen years before he assumed the chairmanship in 1971, using much of his time for oversight of health issues, including one year spent examining the Food and Drug Administration and the structure and programs of the National Institutes of Health.

REENGINEERING: THE YOUNG TURKS

Sam Rayburn (D-Tex.), chairman of the Commerce Committee, 1931-1937, before he became House Majority Leader and, later, Speaker, refashioned the committee to make its jurisdiction equal to his ambitions.

A major supporter of the New Deal, he was instrumental in the passage of bills that established the Securities and Exchange Commission and the Federal Communications Commission. He also authored the Rural Electrification Act. Oren Harris (D-Ark.), advancing to the chairmanship in 1957, brought continued power and prestige to the committee. Harris was perhaps best known for holding oversight hearings on the radio Payola Scandal as well as for his authorship of the Kefauver-Harris Amendments of 1962, which required that drugs be shown to be effective, and not merely safe, before they could be marketed.*

Rogers' skill in presenting ideas and issues in a palatable manner is reflected in his first action upon becoming chairman in 1971. He knew the committee's very title put limits on its jurisdiction. "Public Health" connoted healthcare that was outside the private sector. "Welfare" emphasized that this healthcare was the product of benevolence. It was not where Rogers wanted to go.

Rogers also recognized the environmental movement as a rapidly growing force in the land. It took only a small stretch to link the environment to health and ensure that his committee responsibilities reflected his commitment to environmental laws. So Rogers requested a name change, from the Subcommittee on Public Health and Welfare to the Subcommittee on Health and the Environment. Committee members smiled their approval. With a simple switch of terms, their chairman had expanded their portfolio.

Democrat Harley O. Staggers, a soft-spoken, almost shy, former sheriff and high school and college basketball coach from West Virginia, was now head of the full Commerce Committee. Although his demeanor was unassuming, Staggers' grip over committee and subcommittee activities was suffocating and his vision rarely extended beyond the Mountain State, railroads, coal, and union matters.

Like Rayburn and Harris before him, Staggers sought to rule the committee in dictatorial fashion. The issues to be aired at hearings, the

---

* Actually, the 1962 act responded to the concern not with efficacy but with safety—the damage to fetuses whose mothers had taken thalidomide. In the end, however, the FDA's implementation of the law was hampered by its inability to determine what drugs were on the market.

rooms and times assigned to hear testimony, the parceling out of subcommittee resources (even the stationery), and the fate of legislation were all subject to his approval. Two years after he became chairman of the health subcommittee, Rogers and other activists on the committee engineered a coup. One seed for the revolt was a three-page memo from one of Rogers' staff on the use of drugs and steroids by athletes, most of them professionals. The report was based on interviews with lawyers and athletes in California who spoke in detail about pharmaceutical shopping lists, the use of painkillers, and the routine distribution of barbiturates and amphetamines to athletes. Without revealing his sources, Rogers asked Congressman Bill Roy (D-Kans.), a physician and member of the health subcommittee, to take a look at the pharmacy receipts of an NFL team. A stunned Dr. Roy reported, "You could medicate half the people in Kansas with this!"

Rogers passed on his findings to Staggers, seeking permission to hold hearings on the extent of drug abuse in professional sports. Staggers showed little enthusiasm for pursuing the matter. He would talk to his staff on the Oversight and Investigations Subcommittee,* he said, ending the meeting.

After an appropriate wait, Rogers phoned Staggers. The chairman assured Rogers that his investigator, a former FBI agent, was handling the matter. Now the Rogers office found themselves fearing that Staggers had taken over the story and would break it on his own. And with good reason: Staggers had placed an announcement in the *Congressional Record* that his Oversight Subcommittee would launch an investigation into drug abuse and athletics, thereby preempting any action by Rogers and his subcommittee. But there was no follow-through on Staggers' part. His Oversight Subcommittee never held hearings or issued a report, and Rogers' investigative work was buried.†

---

* Chairing the Oversight Subcommittee was typically the prerogative of the full committee chairman.

† Ultimately, despite Staggers' inaction, the issue of drugs and athletes made headlines over the next two decades, eventually exploding yet another 10 years later.

The experience was yet another example of Staggers' total control over committee activities. Thus, the die was cast. In 1975, Rogers, together with Democrats John Moss of California and John Dingell of Michigan, supported by members of the Watergate class,* wrested much of the control over subcommittee activities from Staggers. But first, the concept was shopped throughout the majority side. Those senior committee members who had shown a desire for a more active agenda met to examine a draft proposal for reallocating jurisdiction. They redrafted the committee rules to apportion subcommittee chairmanships among themselves and provide for their own staffs and budgets. By building consensus before approaching Staggers, they were able to present their master plan to him as a fait accompli. If he had put it to a vote, he would have lost. In this way, they gained control over legislative actions within their jurisdiction, and with staff now available, they freed themselves to pursue aggressive subcommittee agendas.

It wasn't too long before the entire Interstate and Foreign Commerce Committee (subsequently renamed the House Energy and Commerce Committee) became a blockbuster panel regulating or deregulating the telephone and cable industries and a substantial part of the nation's financial systems. It also addressed U.S. energy shortages and conservation needs; transportation; consumer protection; and, of course, complex policies affecting health and the environment.

The ability of the Commerce Committee to exert a profound effect on so many issues stems in good measure from Rogers' early vision of the committee's potential. He had total confidence in his peers, and they in him. But he realized that facing off against a full committee chairman was a radical act. A chairman represented the seniority system, the cornerstone of the House's organizational base. Rogers' ability to know just how far to

---

* The Watergate class was made up of activist congressmen first elected in 1974, many of whom had pledged during their campaigns to throw out the Old Guard. One of the reforms they advanced called for full committee chairs to be elected by the entire caucus of the majority party and for subcommittee chairs to be elected by members of the majority party on the full committee, rather than according to the House seniority-system protocol. Under this procedure, Staggers lost his chairmanship of the Oversight and Investigations Subcommittee to Moss.

go to accomplish change and yet not make it appear radical allowed him to accomplish his goals without creating enmity. In this low-key manner, all his colleagues became shareholders in the potential for change. He continued to establish trust and respect among his peers. His was leadership without bluster.

Chapter 2

Win Some, Lose Some

In each session of Congress, thousands of bills are introduced. Many are new; others are left over from inaction during the previous session. Most are never passed into law.*

Congressional hearings are not limited to consideration of legislation however. They can also involve oversight of a law's implementation or of a general issue under a committee's sphere of jurisdiction.

Under almost any criterion, the bulging portfolio of public law Paul Rogers passed during his tenure in the House of Representatives marks him as one of the most successful legislators in that chamber. The more than 50 laws he brought to fruition affected the entire spectrum of health, including the biomedical research underlying new treatments; the burgeoning field of genetics; regulation of food, drugs, and medical devices; education of healthcare professionals; expansion of health services; extension of consumer education and rights to patients; and setting standards for environmental health. He also spotlighted health and environmental issues through carefully orchestrated oversight hearings.

---

* John Dingell (D-Mich.), Rogers' longtime friend and eventually a chairman of the full Commerce Committee, reintroduces his national health insurance bill each session. His bill is identical to the bill his father had authored before him with no chance of enactment.

It is certainly plausible that only Rogers, with his credentials from the conservative South and moderate voting record, could create, expand, and move Federal health programs the way he did. His personality complemented his professional demeanor. Members on both sides of the aisle not only liked him personally, but soon came to agree with him that health and environmental legislation was important to constituents. Furthermore, Rogers' legislation could be defended back home, even in the most conservative district.

Unlike Senator Kennedy (D-Mass.) or the Clinton White House, Rogers never mounted a full-scale crusade to address or change the nation's healthcare system in toto. Instead, he addressed the nation's health status by developing programs, step by step, aimed at making minor but significant changes in key sectors of the healthcare system. As he became increasingly concerned about deficiencies in health care, all the laws he developed or helped enact were bound by a common, unstated principle, namely, that the Federal government has a role to play in the quality and availability of healthcare in America.

To openly state such a principle in the early '70s would have been totally out of character for Rogers and might have truncated his successes, if not his career. By moving gradually, without great lurches, he rarely alarmed the proponents of the status quo. Nevertheless, he helped change the landscape of healthcare in America and frequently led the charge, too. A few examples follow.

MENTAL HEALTH

Concern over mental health has been long-standing in the United States, where the majority of mental health patients were once treated in state hospitals. But evidence started building in the '50s that these patients were being kept heavily sedated and that the odds of their ever leaving a mental hospital after two years were next to none. As a nation, we were warehousing our mentally ill with little hope of their ever returning to society as productive citizens. As we came to know that many patients can benefit from living at or near home and being treated close by, and that psychotropic drugs can help many do so, it became obvious that sedation alone was not a substitute for treatment. A similar pattern of institutionalization prevailed with regard to people with developmental disabilities. The Mental Retardation Facilities and Community Mental Health Centers Construction Act, 1963, an initiative of President Kennedy, sponsored by Rogers on the House side and Ted Kennedy on the Senate side, triggered the deinstitutionalization movement for people who would do better living in the community like other people. Community mental health services started to spring up across the nation, serving patients on both an inpatient and an outpatient basis.

> **ON RUNNING SCARED**
>
> Paul Rogers told me this story: One time a Congressman came in and said to him, "Paul, I'm so worried, I'm trying to support your work on the Clean Air Act, but the auto workers are all over me in my district, and they are big contributors to my campaign. What can you help me do?" After the guy left, Paul said, " If I had to run scared like that, I wouldn't run anymore."
>
> —Professional staffer Jeff Schwartz

GENETICS AND DISEASE

The National Sickle Cell Anemia Control Act, 1972, addressed the imbalance of research funding for illnesses of specific ethnic groups. The impact of these laws went beyond their primary mission; they also served to call public attention to the need for increased biomedical research. The act provided resources for treatment of and research into a genetic problem limited, almost exclusively, to African Americans. Amendments included in a bill sponsored by Paul Rogers in 1976 extended the law to other genetic diseases, including Cooley's anemia (thalassemia), which primarily affects people of Mediterranean, African, and Southeastern Asian ancestry, and Tay Sachs disease, which affects Jewish people of Eastern European descent.

DRUG ABUSE TREATMENT AND PREVENTION

A primary focus of President Nixon's law-and-order administration was the war on drugs, with law enforcement and treatment efforts scattered throughout the Executive Branch. A White House initiative in 1971 established a Special Action Office for Drug Abuse Prevention to coordinate the nation's drug-abuse prevention activities. Rogers cosponsored the legislation in the House, with an amendment approved by Nixon, to establish the offices within the White House and be responsible to the President, and led its passage through Congress. Thus, the nation's first Drug Czar was established. The bill never achieved its objective, because the new office did not get responsibility for the budgets of the agencies it was to coordinate.*

SAFE DRINKING WATER

Former Rogers professional staffer Jeff Schwartz recalls Rogers' struggle to get the Safe Drinking Water Act of 1974—the nation's first—passed.

> Roger's determination to get things done showed up in all kinds of ways. I worked on one bill that I think Rogers deserves a lot of credit for, the first Federal safe drinking water act. Although a Federal safe food act had been in effect since 1906, water was not regulated at the Federal level except on interstate conveyances, such as trains and airplanes. Rogers got this bill through the committee with a great deal of difficulty. It then got hung up in the Rules Committee, and Rogers couldn't get a rule, meaning the bill was not eligible for a vote on the House floor. It turned out that B.F. Sisk (D-Calif.), a member of the Rules Committee, was upset because a bill reimbursing hospitals for the care of immigrants that was important to his district was not moving out of the Rogers committee. As far as Sisk was concerned, he was not about to help Rogers get a bill through until Rogers took care of his bill. I just couldn't figure out why we couldn't get it through the Rules Committee, and Steve Lawton said to me, "Why don't we go and talk to Sisk's guy?" Sisk's guy was Tony Coelho, who succeeded Sisk as a congressman from California. I went to him and explained that I was new on the Hill and didn't understand how these things work, but that Congressman Sisk seems to have a problem with the Safe Drinking Water Bill. "I'm not sure I understand what it is. Could you help me?" Coelho looked at me in disbelief and said, "What don't you understand? The problem is that your congressman is not letting my congressman's bill get a hearing. Between us, it's unlikely that your bill will get a rule unless our bill moves almost immediately." Rogers held a hearing on Sisk's bill—which had no chance of passage—so that the Safe Drinking Water Bill, in turn, could get through. That was the first step.

---

* The Golden Rule = He who controls the gold, rules. This was relearned by Congress in 2004 as it tried to establish a single national intelligence agency.

The Safe Drinking Water Bill was not a favorite of the Republicans. What was the Federal government doing regulating water supply at local and state levels? After Paul got it on the House calendar, one of the Republicans stood up on the House floor and warned, "There are going to be Federal inspectors coming out of every tap in every home in the world as a result of this bill."

Rogers still got the bill passed, but now President Ford was reluctant to sign it because of Republican pressure. Rogers worked it out. He found a way to get his bill into an omnibus bill that included other measures that Senator Orrin Hatch (R-Utah) wanted.* Hatch, even then influential with other Senate Republicans, became an advocate for the total bill even if not of the Safe Drinking Water Act portion. The law has resulted in the upgrade of hundreds of drinking-water systems across the country. In addition, the Federal Superfund law used one of the act's drinkable-water standards for cleaning up toxic waste sites, resulting in the EPA setting valuable standards to protect public health.

At one point, Rogers, who usually does not get worked up, did get frustrated by his own committee's refusal to understand the importance of the Clean Water Bill. It was during the Arab oil embargo. I remember Rogers, during a committee hearing, picking up a pitcher of water and exclaiming, "If you think Americans are mad when they go to their gas pumps but can't get any gas for their cars, think how they are going to feel when they go to their faucets and they can't get any water to drink." Nobody had an answer to that. He had a way of dramatizing things simply and clearly that communicated powerfully.

HEALTH CARE DELIVERY AND COST CONTAINMENT

By the mid-1970s, health care costs in the United States were skyrocketing at double-digit levels, raising concern within Congress and the Executive Branch. Two Congressional responses bear Rogers' name: One is the Health Maintenance Organization Act, 1973, which promised grants and contracts to nonprofit entities to encourage the establishment of HMOs and which also required employers to include HMO services among the health coverage options they offered to their employees. Rogers and his colleagues saw the

* Typically, at the end of a congressional session, Congress passes an omnibus bill that bundles up several independent pieces of legislation.

HMO concept—with its emphasis on preventative care and an offering medical services at a fixed, capitated rate, rather than on a fee-for-service basis—as a way to improve health status while controlling costs.

The second legislative effort was the health planning law. Its premise was that new Federal agencies were necessary to complement and, to some extent, supplant the work of state comprehensive planning agencies. The Health Planning and Resources Development Act, 1975, established Federally funded Health Systems Agencies responsible for planning a more rational growth of health services within the areas they served. The law included some monies for development of new health services, but its primary mission was to have agencies review and determine the need for capital expenditures, institutional health services, and major medical equipment. States were required to beef up their certificate-of-need laws to conform to the HSA's plans.

Neither law had a happy ending. Most HMOs funded under the 1973 law collapsed in the face of a national movement toward for-profit HMOs (now managed care entities). Health-systems agencies, never a favorite of governors, met their demise during the Reagan Revolution. Moreover, legislation proposing cost-containment of hospitals was defeated in the Commerce Committee toward the end of Rogers' tenure. In spite of escalating health costs, Congress was more comfortable with building the country's health system piece by piece than adopting comprehensive strategies to constrain costs.

IONIZING RADIATION

In 1968, as a member (but not chairman) of the House Health Subcommittee, Rogers coauthored the bill that became the Radiation Control for Health and Safety Act. The act required the Food and Drug Administration to address the effects of ionizing radiation on health. The fact that you wear a lead apron when you get a dental X-ray and that a microwave oven shuts down if the door is opened before the timer goes off are direct results of the act. Years later, as head of the health subcommittee, Rogers would take on a more serious radiation problem: namely, the health effects of radioactive discharges from nuclear submarines and the fallout from atomic bombs over western states.

Medical Radiation

The Radiation Control Act actually started with an eight-paragraph story on the second page of the *Miami Herald*'s local section that reported a talk given by a retired investment banker at a woman's organization. The speaker, John Ott, had been experimenting with time-lapse photography as a hobby, and his presentation was on how light rays can alter the growth of flowers. During the discussion afterward, Ott mentioned that he thought his color television set was emitting radiation that could influence the behavior of children sitting close to the screen. He was also conducting research with mice, he said, and noted that on a number of occasions when he inadvertently left the color TV on in his home lab, their behavior changed.*

IT'S ALL RELATIVE, PART 1

Jim Menger, general counsel of the House Interstate and Foreign Commerce Committee when Paul Rogers first came on board, had also been a colleague of the elder Rogers. Asked about the similarities between father and son, Menger didn't hesitate to answer. "Compared with his father, Paul is downright grumpy. Dwight Sr. was one of the nicest men to ever serve on the committee or in the House. He was a very gentle man. Everyone loved him."

In a district that encompassed nearly 900,000 people, it was not unusual to get a call or a letter from a constituent about aliens aiming X-ray beams at him to control his mind. But Ott seemed to have done some creditable work on light rays, and his hypothesis about TV and radiation deserved a follow-up.

Rogers asked the Public Health Service to run some tests. The results validated Ott's observations. Color TVs were indeed leaking measurable amounts of radiation. So were the microwave ovens in employee break rooms. With the microwave oven, there was also concern about cataracts and effects on pacemakers. The ovens had no cut-off mechanism if they

* Ott's time-lapse sequences appeared in a number of Walt Disney nature documentaries. Ott is also credited with identifying the importance of full-spectrum lighting, i.e., all visible light waves, from infrared to ultraviolet.

were opened before the timer went off; they just kept going and going. Other radiation-generating equipment also posed potential health risks. Dental X-ray equipment, for example, was crudely calibrated and shipped with no indication that it should be checked and recalibrated periodically.

As a result of the Radiation Control Act, oversight of health-safety controls in radiation-emitting products shifted from the Bureau of Radiological Health of the Public Health Service to the Food and Drug Administration in 1971. The newly formed Environmental Protection Agency took over environmental radiation. Microwave ovens were thereafter manufactured with protective seals and cutoffs, the entire field of possible damage from X rays was spotlighted, and manufacturers of several other products were made aware of the need to design or redesign potentially harmful products with safety in mind. Once the product leaves the manufacturer, the enforcement of safety standards is left to states and municipalities; the laws are a somewhat uneven mix but, by and large, extremely stringent.

Nuclear Radiation

By the mid-1970s, Rogers' reputation for fairness was known throughout the health and environment communities. Even his opponents appreciated his willingness to listen to both sides of an issue and hold a fair hearing. Treated with respect, they responded in kind. There were a few exceptions, and Paul Rogers was eventually to meet one: Admiral Hyman Rickover. In early 1978, the father of the nuclear navy was called in to testify during Rogers' hearing on the health effects of nuclear radiation.

Public concern had been escalating over the nuclear radiation issue since 1977, when Dr. Thomas Mancuso, an occupational health researcher at the University of Pittsburgh, reported that a quarter-million American servicemen had suffered radiation illnesses after working too close to nuclear-bomb testing sites. The Atomic Energy Commission (subsequently to become part of the Department of Energy), which had contracted for the Mancuso report, rejected the findings and refused to fund the project further. Rogers' committee started looking into the matter in January 1978. By the time Rickover appeared before the committee, the inquiry had expanded into looking at a second study, this one of workers at the

THE DOOR IS ALWAYS OPEN

"Face time" with the boss is lifeblood for a congressional assistant. It is usually in great demand and short supply. On the Hill, it also nourishes egos and enforces feelings of self-worth.

One afternoon, when an administrative assistant to Rogers had settled the details of an opening statement with another congressman's aide, the latter asked: "When will you know if Rogers approves the language?"

"He's out right now, but he'll be back shortly," Rogers' staffer replied.

"You'll see him?"

"Sure."

"Do you see him often?"

"Sure"

"How often?"

"Four, five, ten times a day. Why?"

"Well, what do you have to do to see him?"

"I walk through that door."

"Really? You just walk in? I almost never see my boss."

Portsmouth Naval Shipyard in New Hampshire, where nuclear submarines were serviced and refitted.*

Dr. Thomas Najarian, a hematologist at Boston Veteran's Hospital, had found that the leukemia rate among the Portsmouth workers exposed to radiation was four times higher than average. His research, initially paid for by Najarian himself but later funded by the *Boston Globe*, also found that the exposed workers had a death rate twice the national average and nearly four-fifths higher than shipyard workers who did no nuclear work. The study results had implications for all nuclear shipyard workers and possibly the crews of

* Rogers had a second motive for bringing in Rickover. The admiral would surely attract press coverage, thereby providing the public with information on the nuclear radiation issue.

nuclear vessels. The Navy, having at first denied there was any trouble at Portsmouth, suddenly decided to conduct its own study and asked the Department of Energy to handle it. Rogers felt that Centers for Disease Control and Prevention at the Department of Health, Education, and Welfare, with its expertise in radiation, would conduct a more credible investigation.

Meanwhile, Rickover seemed determined to glide silently under the radar like one of his beloved vessels. But the man hailed as a genius in military journals and the popular press made a tactical error the day he entered the hearing room. The four-star admiral was not pleased to be summoned by a civilian subcommittee with no obvious jurisdiction over any of the operations he commanded. No matter what the circumstance, any uniformed officer knows "the drill on the Hill": Show proper respect for elected civilians. Rickover, however, thought that bluster would cow the panel members.

Rogers, in turn, had just learned, to his great surprise, that Rickover, the man in charge of the nuclear propulsion division of the Navy's Bureau of Ships, was also a manager at the Department of Energy. Thus, Rickover had a vested interest in the outcome of any DOE study.

Rogers: Admiral, do you also hold a position with the Department of Energy?

Rickover: Yes, sir.

Rogers: What is your position at the Department of Energy?

Rickover: To tell you the truth, I do not know.

Rogers asked a witness accompanying Rickover to explain the admiral's work at DOE. Rickover interjected: "I'll tell you what I think it is." He outlined his duties, but not his position.

Rogers asked how much time Rickover spent at the two agencies. Rickover replied, "I do not think you can make a line distinction. It is all mixed up."

Rogers: Well, I think we could divide it. Do you have an office over there?

Rickover: No. No.

Rogers: Do you have a separate staff to handle DOE?

Rickover: No sir. One staff [TRANSCRIPT UNCLEAR].

Rogers: I just want to be clear. You operate out of your Navy office, but you have this position you hold at DOE?

Rickover: I have an office in the Energy Building, also.

Rogers: One staff. None are on the Energy payroll?

Rickover: Some are on the Energy payroll and some are on the Navy's.

Rogers: That is what I want to know.

Rickover: Some are military, some are civilian. I do not know who they are.

Rogers: Who does know?

Rickover: I guess we have a record.

Rogers: (livid) Well, I would hope so, Admiral. I do not want to appear to be absurd, but you are talking now to a committee of the Congress, and we are asking how you operate. Now I would hope you would be responsive.

(enunciating each word clearly) If not, then we can adjourn this hearing and let you go back and get the information or someone who can provide answers to our questions. Is that clear?

Rickover: Yes, sir. I am really being as responsive as I can.

Rogers: Well, I would not have anticipated that from your answers to any questions.

The hearing room went quiet. Some people looked down out of embarrassment. Rogers was breathing hard. It took close to five minutes for him to calm down. Rickover asked permission to add to and correct the record.

Rogers: Certainly.

Rickover: May I have your permission to leave now, unless you have more questions?

Rogers: (making it clear who was running this show) I may have a question or two more, thank you. We will try to conclude as soon as possible.

In the end, Rickover conceded. He accepted the committee's decision that the Centers for Disease Control should evaluate Najarian's findings. But the end was not in sight. The CDC referred responsibility for the study to the National Institute for Occupational Safety and Health. The findings were inconclusive. NIOSH submitted its results for publication without ever presenting them to Rogers' committee. The health issues raised during the hearings were never resolved, and the congressional inquiry ended with a fizzle. Today, responsibility for worker protection from ionizing radiation resides in several regulatory agencies, Federal (e.g., the Nuclear Regulatory Commission and the Environmental Protection Agency), state, and local.

THE OZONE LAYER

In December 1974, the Rogers committee started hearings on the findings of two college professors—F. Sherwood Rowland and Mario Molina—who had published a study in *Nature* suggesting that chlorofluorocarbons (CFCs), once released, rose in the atmosphere and tore into the ozone layer, allowing an unusual number of ultraviolet rays to hit our planet, theoretically contributing to raising Earth's temperature and causing skin cancer. Yet, if you looked around, people were not falling over dead. Instead, they kept cool, their hair stayed in place, and they smelled better. The concept of these apparently benign chemicals poking a hole in the ozone layer seemed like choice material for TV's *Rowan and Martin's Laugh-In*, not for a congressional inquiry.

Rogers' staff urged him to become the first in Congress to hold Hill oversight hearings on CFCs. They argued that otherwise, the research could be buried in scientific journals or even be picked up by another legislator. If

Rogers held the hearings, they argued, the CFC theory would be seen as plausible. If somebody else—say, a liberal from New York or California—were to hold the first hearing, the concern over CFCs will be easily dismissed.

CFC is a synthetic component that was used as a coolant in refrigerators and air-conditioning systems, a propellant in aerosol sprays, and a cleanser for electronic components. The two researchers had found that CFCs remained stable in the lower atmosphere but began to break down at extremely high altitudes; here the released chlorine from CFCs could start a chain reaction, with a single chlorine atom wiping out hundreds of ozone molecules.

Rogers moved quickly. The research was not yet at a stage where CFC damage could be proven, so he knew better than to open the hearing with gloom and doom. He called in a blue-ribbon list of scientists to validate Rowland and Molina's work.* Witnesses from DuPont, the largest producer of CFCs, however, were not fully convinced of the science underlying the CFC studies or of any threat posed by CFCs.

Rogers: What if the science does prove out? Would you still produce your product?

DuPont: We believe that Roland and Molina's theory has no scientific basis. If it did, we would stop selling these chlorinated fluorocarbons in aerosol cans.

Rogers: Good. But how do we get to know if Rowland and Molina's theory is right or not? Is there any chlorine in your product? If the chlorine was free, could it affect the ozone layer?

DuPont: Well, yes, theoretically. But that's the brilliance of this product. It is stable.

---

* As the hearings progressed, Rogers' staff was stunned and bewildered by a sudden outpouring of support from music fans. The rock band Commander Cody and the Ozone Patrol heard about Rogers' efforts and at every concert distributed save-the-ozone postcards. The audience filled them out and mailed them to Rogers' office by the bagful. Staff kept track of where Commander Cody was performing by the postmarks.

Other industry witnesses put in their word. They said there was no substitute for the CFCs. In any event, removing CFCs was not technologically feasible; and, moreover, it would cost too much if it could be done at all.

In 1976, the National Academy of Sciences confirmed the Rowland and Molina findings. In 1978, the United States, Canada, Denmark, Norway, and Sweden banned the use of CFCs in aerosol sprays. In the mid-1980s, scientists discovered a hole in the ozone-shield over Antarctica. In 1987, the United Nations called for a ban on all ozone-damaging gases by 1996. The industry stopped producing chlorofluorocarbons in 1995. Rowland and Molina received a Nobel Prize for their work that same year. Rogers' oversight hearings had served their purpose: protection of the public health.*

THE HEALTH WORKFORCE

One of Rogers' many passions on the Hill concerned the health workforce, particularly the geographic maldistribution of health professionals (too many in the suburbs, not enough in rural or difficult urban areas), and the specialty maldistribution of physicians (too many specialists, not enough primary care doctors).

Serving the Underserved

Jarman's deferral on health issues had helped put Rogers' image on the health community's radar; his colleagues in the Senate also took note. For Rogers, running the hearings was satisfying and rewarding. It also whet his appetite for more. So the congressman was delighted when Senator Warren Magnuson (D-Wash.) asked him to review and be the House sponsor of a legislative proposal for a national health service corps pledged to serve in a medically "underserved" or "need" area for a specified period of time in return for Federal scholarships or loan-forgiveness.

* When amendments to the Clean Air Act were introduced in 1977, Rogers seized the opportunity to insert a provision that provided for a study on cumulative effects of all substances that may affect the ozone layer, as well as for a study on the effects on industry of a ban on the use of halocarbons (including CFCs) in aerosol containers.

The bill faced considerable opposition from organized medicine and the Nixon Administration. Rogers, however, took hold of it and made it his. The legislation would strengthen the existing health care system, Rogers explained to foes of the legislation, because its focus was on locations shunned by most health caregivers. Neither would the new doctors be there forever, he argued, although the hope was that, after having fulfilled their obligation, many would stay on in private practice. He also added a provision that the Department of Health, Education, and Welfare (now Health and Human Services) would certify that an area was underserved, but the local medical association would have a say, too. He designed a provision to overcome state problems with state licensure laws. The conservative from Florida also increased the funding from the Senate's version of $15 million to $60 million. And as a result of Rogers' prodding, Dr. Tim Lee Carter (R-Ky.), the committee member who had charged that the bill was setting up government doctors in America's health system, turned around to become a co-sponsor of the bill.

Operating in a lame duck session, the Commerce Committee and the House easily passed the Emergency Health Personnel Act, 1970. In conference, most of the provisions Rogers had added were adopted. The Administration, however, had opposed the bill throughout its journey, and it wasn't about to let go now. Vice President Agnew, as the Senate's presiding officer, used his muscle to delay Senate action. This maneuver gave President Nixon the option to pocket-veto the bill. Otherwise he would either have to sign it into law one day before Congress was scheduled to adjourn, or veto it directly and risk a congressional override of a popular bill. But Rogers and Magnuson conspired to tell interested parties that they had received permission to hold Congress in session for one more day, making a pocket veto impossible. Nixon signed the bill on the final day of the 91st Congress. It was the last bill passed in that session, and the first ever to establish a government healthcare service outside of the traditional jurisdiction of the Public Health Service.*

---

* It is one of the most successful health programs ever established, with close to 25,000 healthcare providers having served with the Corps by 2004.

Augmenting Health Professions Education

In tackling health workforce issues, Rogers developed a strong understanding for academic medicine, and a fondness as well. He found the field to be similar in many ways to politics on Capitol Hill.* During the 1970s, medical and other health professions schools received massive Federal funding from HEW in addition to funding from the National Institutes of Health. Most of it was the result of health workforce laws enacted in 1971 and 1976 under Rogers' leadership. The Association of Medical Colleges, the Association of Academic Health Centers, and many medical school deans were heavily involved in crafting these laws, thereby forging a partnership between the Federal government and health professions educators.

Increasing the National Healthcare Workforce

A primary premise of the Health Professionals Education Assistance Act passed in 1971 was that there was a national shortage of physicians and other health professionals. It, therefore, provided a quid pro quo: In return for capitation grants (monies to schools based on numbers of students enrolled), schools were required to increase enrollment. Grants were also available to start new medical schools and convert two-year schools into full, four-year programs.

This landmark law also authorized funding for myriad special projects, ranging from area health-education centers for training medical students and residents in shortage areas to primary-care teaching programs for nurse practitioners. It was well funded by congressional appropriators, thanks in no small part to the efforts of many politically astute medical school deans. It resulted ultimately in the construction of several new health professions schools and expansion of many more. A corollary to this law was the Nurse Training Act, 1971, which used capitation grants, loans, loan-forgiveness, and scholarships to promote nurse-training, including increased responsibilities for patient care.

---

* Chief Counsel Steve Lawton once remarked, "The politics of academic medicine makes Cook County politics seem like child's play."

By the mid 1970s, many people in the healthcare field doubted there was indeed a shortage of health professionals.* Attention now turned to specialty and geographic maldistribution—a problem with significantly more political implications than sheer increases in numbers merely increasing the overall number of healthcare professionals in the country. Nevertheless, Rogers' Health Professions Educational Assistance Act, 1976, made it through Congress, authorizing a significant expansion of the National Health Service Corps and massive funding of primary-care teaching programs.

Overcoming Specialty Imbalances

Rogers' efforts to combat specialty maldistribution resulted in one of only two of Rogers' defeats on the House floor† during his eight-year tenure as chairman of the Health and Environment Subcommittee. He proposed a program regulating entry into first-year medical residency programs by requiring that, ultimately, 50 percent of first-year positions be in the primary care specialties (family medicine, general internal medicine, and pediatrics). Blindsided by the American Medical Association, Rogers' proposal for Federal regulation of entry into medical residency training was easily defeated by a Republican motion to strike. It would be left to the hiring practices of managed-care organizations a decade later to correct the inequity.

MEDICAL DEVICES

In the 1970s, American consumers had little confidence, and rightly so, that the increasingly sophisticated medical devices now on the market were safe and effective. Significant injuries, and even deaths, for example, were reported as a result of faulty pacemakers and damaging IUDs (intrauterine devices), which gained market entry without Food and Drug Administration review. The FDA had responded by treating some medical devices as drugs in the only way they could, requiring that the devices undergo clinical trials and

---

* Rogers himself was never convinced that the United States had sufficient physicians, constantly recounting constituent complaints that "I can't find a doctor."

† The other was failure to defeat John Dingell's amendment to reduce automobile emission standards under the Clean Air Act Amendments in 1977 (chapter 3).

approval. Only after the pharmaceutical industry lost two lawsuits challenging the FDA's authority in this matter were the manufacturers ready to deal. Together, the pharmaceutical industry and the FDA crafted a bill that easily passed the Senate. Most lobbyists urged the House members to follow suit because the bill represented an agreement between industry and the government. But Rogers decided that the bill needed more careful scrutiny.

The Senate-proposed legislation had adopted recommendations made by Dr. Theodore Cooper, while head of what was then the National Heart and Lung Institute, that medical devices be classified in one of three categories depending on potential risk: Class I, Premarket Approval based on clinical studies; Class II, Standards to which a device would conform; or Class III, General Controls, such as requirements for labeling and proper manufacturing.

Rogers, although a keen supporter of the FDA, believed that its drug-review officers were prone to overregulation, causing a long lag time before pharmaceutical products reached the consumer. He ordered his staff to redraft the Senate bill with a subtle distinction: invert the classification system so that the third type of regulation available (General Controls) fell into the first category; keep Standards as the second option; and make Premarket Approval the third category. He also directed the insertion of a new requirement, namely, that only the least category of regulation "necessary to reasonably assure that the device be safe and effective" be imposed by the FDA. In so doing, he protected consumers from risky medical devices, yet still allowed innovative, life-saving products to enter the U.S. marketplace within a reasonable time. With these simple changes, he was also able to respond to the increasingly antiregulatory atmosphere that was beginning to emerge in Congress.*

The new law, the Medical Device Amendments of 1976, was the most important revision to food and drug law since the Kefauver-Harris Amendments of 1962.

---

* Even before he became subcommittee chairman, Rogers had chaired oversight hearings inquiring into bottlenecks at the FDA that delayed approval of new drugs. During protracted hearings, drug companies had detailed long delays in moving new drug applications through the FDA. Rogers discovered that agency personnel reviewing data on drug trials were requesting additional information from the manufacturer at the end of the mandated 180-day deadline for a decision on an application. Such requests would "restart the clock."

Following the successful rewrite of this law, Rogers turned to recasting the FDA's authority over drugs and to giving FDA authority to write consumer-oriented patient-package inserts, but this was seen by industry as a threat to the bond between physicians and drug "detail men" (salespeople). In fact, industry mounted a court challenge to FDA's authority to require patient-package inserts at all, but lost—making a new law unnecessary.

In 1978 Rogers introduced hundreds of pages of legislation drafted by FDA and his committee staff proposing a massive rewrite of FDA's drug authority. But enthusiasm for the several-hundred page bill waned in Congress upon Rogers' retirement.

In other instances, staff, after having nearly completed a review, would be suddenly reassigned, and their replacements had to begin the review process all over again. The nub of the problem finally became apparent. The thalidomide disaster in 1968 had so shaken the corps of skilled and dedicated FDA professionals that no one wanted to sign off on a drug if there was any possible chance it could do harm.

Chapter 3

A Study in Contrasts

Of all of Paul Rogers' legislative efforts in the 1970s, two stand out as high-impact, high-visibility, high-stakes legislation: the 1977 Amendments to the original Clean Air Act (1970), and the National Cancer Act, 1971.

The Clean Air Act contained the first congressionally mandated automobile-emission standards: a 90 percent reduction in three pollutants by 1975. Like many of the bills under Rogers' aegis, it required periodic congressional review to determine if adjustments were needed. The 1975 review of the Clean Air Act precipitated a no-holds-barred, two-year brawl on the floors of both the House of Representatives and the Senate. On one side were the automobile manufacturers, chemical companies, utility companies, petroleum refiners and distributors, the coal industry, and paper and steel industries. The stakes to industry were big, possibly hundreds of millions of dollars in pollution-control costs. Facing off were the "tree-huggers" (as their detractors called them) representing all the environmental groups, plus the heart, lung, and cancer advocacy groups. Aging constituencies, mayors, counties, state legislators, and governors also had a stake in the outcome, one way or another. And the two unions most heavily involved with automobile and steel production—the United Auto Workers and the United Steel Workers of America—did a legislative dance worthy of any

United Nations diplomat. Each side clung to its position, convinced that to give an inch meant defeat.

In contrast, the battle for the legislation that created the National Cancer Act was fought by well-intended, politically connected power players; distinguished men and women of science; and Ann Landers, the nationally syndicated columnist. Unlike the unruly clean air battle, the process surrounding establishing the cancer act was fought under Marquess of Queensbury rules. Egos, not fortunes, were at stake. Fighting cancer was a motherhood issue.

THE CLEAN AIR ACT

During the five years since the original Clean Air Act set automobile-emissions standards, a mass of evidence had accumulated demonstrating the damaging effect of air pollution on humans, crops, wildlife, and the environment. Headlines screamed "Mutant Fish," "Two-Headed Frogs," and "Acid Rain." Readers searched to see where their city fell on annual most-polluted-cities lists. Volunteer heart and lung societies connected air pollution to asthma, lung disease, and premature death. High levels of lead in newborns were linked to airborne lead particulates. Membership in established environmental and conservation groups boomed and multiplied. Astronauts, peering down at Earth, reported they could identify only two human-made things: the Great Wall of China and the smoke plumes from the Four Corners Power Plant located at the nexus of Arizona, Colorado, New Mexico, and Utah. Rogers sensed that the public's interest and support for environmental issues was increasing at an amazing rate.

Other issues complicated the clean air debate. The OPEC oil embargo and subsequent energy crisis had created long gas lines and higher prices. Prices also rose on many everyday products, based in part on the cost of petrochemical feedstock. All this sent a ripple through the U.S. economy as inflation and interest rates neared all-time highs.

Cheap, high-mileage Japanese cars started eating away at the American market share at an alarming rate. A requirement for cleaner automobile emissions at this time could drive up the cost of American cars further and decrease fuel efficiency. Cleaner power plants might mean expensive new scrubber technology or the elimination of cheap coal; the latter required plants to convert to more expensive oil or natural gas.

Meanwhile, under the Energy Policy and Conservation Act, 1975, Congress had established corporate average fuel economy (CAFE) standards, requiring automakers to produce more fuel-efficient cars. Detroit manufacturers planned to leverage the demands CAFE had saddled them with to soften the growing chorus for cleaner air. Additionally, automakers predicted that lowering emissions further would decrease fuel efficiency and that the necessary technology was both unproven and expensive. Finally, they persuaded their largest union, the United Auto Workers, that jobs would be lost.

KNOW THEM BY THE COMPANY THEY KEEP

We used to say that you could tell a member of Congress by his staff, and you could know the character of staff by looking at the person they worked for. In Paul Rogers' case, the result was a slightly driven, hard-working, decent, public-spirited cast of characters who liked each other and wanted to make a difference in the world.

—Professional staffer Jeff Schwartz

Many congressional districts had a power plant, a chemical plant, a refinery, a paper mill, or at the least, a smelter. The managers or owners usually knew their representatives in Congress. The 41-member Commerce Committee mirrored the situation. The Clean Air Act amendments required all major new power plants to install the best air-pollution control technology, just as plants undergoing major renovations were required to do under the 1970 provisions. Some thought that changing fuel sources should be an option, or perhaps building taller smokestacks to disperse the pollution. Another division in the committee concerned the use of coal. The problem was that soft coal from the eastern part of the United States was plentiful and less costly than the cleaner, western coal that would be required. If a subcommittee member was from a soft coal state, his constituency was threatened. For hard-coal states, fuel-switching could be a plus.*

* Speaker of the House Tip O'Neill (D-Mass.) once summed it up by saying, "All politics is local."

Nevertheless, Rogers was able to move the Clean Air Bill through both his subcommittee and the full committee without major problems, in part because he not only caught a break, but also knew how to make use of coincidental timing. The young, reform-minded Democrats, "the Watergate class," that the Nixon backlash had brought into Congress, wanted change. A disproportionate number ended up on the Commerce Committee. Rogers included them in the legislative process and earned their trust and respect. They lent heft to the pro-environment cause and made Rogers' position look moderate by comparison. The bill received some Republican support, too, and some issues important to affected business communities were modified.

Now loomed the biggest symbol of clean-air legislation: the automobile-pollutant standards. Industry could not muster the votes to amend them in the bill during the subcommittee vote. However, a seasoned, respected, rough-and-tumble committee member was ready to carry their banner. He was a prominent Democrat, John Dingell from Michigan. The large, lumbering, bespectacled man and Rogers were good friends.* Over the years, few votes on the Commerce Committee separated Rogers and Dingell, although Dingell was a northern liberal and a loyal union advocate.

On the final day of the Clean Air Bill mark-up in the Commerce Committee, Dingell would try to undo what his good friend Rogers had worked so hard to do in subcommittee. Dingell was from Dearborn. In the following months he would be introduced as the "Congressman from Ford." He was on a mission. What's more, he relished a good fight.

Waiting for a quorum to appear, the two men chatted. The hearing room was packed. Rogers called his staff to an anteroom to go over details. Dingell had circulated the amendment he intended to offer, which would ease the automobile-emission requirements. Rogers had prepared a counter amendment to serve as a compromise appeal to subcommittee members who wanted to announce they had voted to provide some relaxation of the

---

* Among the characteristics they had in common were fathers whom they revered, who had been congressmen, and who had died in office. The two men also had daughters about the same age.

original numbers but still vote for a cleaner environment. Dingell popped in to ask, "Do you want to go first or do you want me to offer my amendment first? It doesn't matter to me, Paul."

"Why don't you go first, John," Rogers said without hesitation. Dingell left. An aide asked why Rogers wanted Dingell to go first. "If there is a tie, the amendment loses," Rogers said. The aide, who had been responsible for counting potential votes over the past week, couldn't figure this out. There was an odd number of members on the committee. How could there be a tie vote?

In preparing for key votes on controversial issues, House members, their staffs, and lobbyists contact every voting member to present their case and ask for their vote. The results fall into five categories—yes, leaning yes, no, leaning no, and undecided. Once past the committed ayes and nays, the gambit is to pressure the "leaning" and "undecided" to line up with you. Rogers' public allies had all been assigned House members to talk to and had been asked to report the responses. Extremely important to the process was knowing if a member might or might not be present for the vote. In that case, a signed proxy sheet was acceptable.

Each side scoured the halls and the House floor with proxy sheets, seeking signatures. Committee chairman Harley Staggers had committed his vote to Rogers because he would have to leave the mark-up early. Rogers had his staff collect a proxy from Staggers. This was good, the aide thought, because Staggers was someone vulnerable to last-minute lobbying. It was almost better to have his proxy than his presence. Despite every effort, there remained several members whose votes could not be confidently predicted. It was too close to call.

The debate during mark-up was classic: each side painted grim consequences if the other side won. There was sniping. Ridicule rained down on both sides. Meanwhile, Staggers had left, and John Moss (D-Calif.) had taken the gavel. A vote on the Dingell amendment was called for. Moss ordered the clerk to call the roll.

Relying on weeks of exhaustive canvassing, Rogers had a list of how he thought the votes would go. He checked off each member as he declared. Some members passed their turn and would vote later, elevating the suspense. When his time came, Tim Lee Carter, the ranking minority member of Rogers' committee and a country doctor, voted "Yes." It was a big surprise.

Finally, all committee members present had voted. The proxies were called in. Some members announced they had someone else's proxy and so voted. The clerk, in turn, announced the proxies given to him before and during the debate. He scanned the tally sheet and counted. He started to signal the chairman that he had a total, but Rogers called for the clerk to announce the proxy vote of Staggers. The clerk stared down at the table in front of him. "There is no proxy for Chairman Staggers," he announced.

"Chairman Staggers left his proxy before we began," Rogers said.

"Yes, sir," the clerk replied. "And he took it back when he left."

The room exploded. Rogers had been sabotaged. Dingell broke into a great smile. He turned to Rogers, seated to his right, and slapped his friend's back. The chair brought his wooden gavel down hard to restore order and then ordered the clerk to report the vote. "On the amendment, there are 20 yes's and 20 no's," the clerk said in a monotone voice.

At that moment, few realized what had just transpired. The amendment had failed on a tie vote.

Dingell's face grew pinched. His forehead furrowed. His eyes all but disappeared behind his glasses. The audience again erupted. There was scattered applause. It was possibly the first time in congressional memory that Dingell had lost. Rogers knew better than to offer any form of condolence at that moment.

The full committee passed the bill without other weakening amendments. The press and well-wishers from both the audience and the committee flocked to Rogers. As he was inching out of the committee room, the aide spoke quietly to Rogers. "I didn't know about the Staggers proxy," he said. "I didn't either," Rogers replied.

But Dingell was not finished. Backed by an immense campaign by both industry and labor lobbyists from the automobile industry, Dingell offered his amendment during House debate; it carried by 12 votes. Just prior to the full House vote, Rogers had met with co-sponsor Senator Edmund Muskie (D-Maine), and advised him to make the Senate's version of the bill tougher. In this way, if the Dingell amendment passed the

House, they could negotiate a compromise on the standards in conference. The issue was now to be settled by a House-Senate conference.*

The Senate, led by Muskie, soon passed its version of the bill, and conferees from the two bodies met to reconcile the differences. Dingell's auto amendment was part of the House bill, so he was the House spokesman for that portion. Muskie wanted it out. Here were two proud, hardheaded, stubborn men facing off.

Conferees met and wrangled for several days. The auto-emission standards were at the core of the drama. Each side was uncompromising. Award-winning filmmaker Charles Guggenheim had been chronicling the process for a documentary. Now he was afraid his deadline, even his funds, would not hold out.

One night, past midnight, Muskie exploded. He would walk away from the bill, leaving it to die, rather than compromise on the auto standards. He stalked out of the near-empty room. Guggenheim's camera could not catch the moment. The filmmaker had run out of film hours ago.

Finally, a newly appointed senator, Wendell Anderson (D-Minn.),† joined the fray. At about two o'clock in the morning, Anderson slammed his hand on the table separating the House and the Senate conferees, and said,

> I am new here [to Washington]. On several days, my children cannot go on the playground for recess because of the air pollution. The pollution here must be caused by auto emissions—there are no industrial plants that could cause it. Where are the smokestacks?

Dingell slumped into a lounge chair, exhausted. He would not, he said, stand in the way of passing the bill. Despite severe reservations about the adverse impact of the bill on the automobile industry, he would relent, reluctantly.

---

* The bill that passed the House was not limited to the contested automobile-emission standards. It also called for new power plants to employ the best antipollution technology, thereby wedding the revised act's provisions to the original 1970 act requiring plants undergoing major modification to install such technology.

† Anderson had resigned his position as governor of Minnesota in 1976 when Senator Walter Mondale became vice president. He was then appointed by the new Governor to finish Mondale's term.

Anderson's comments helped carry, and Dingell graciously conceded. He and Rogers shook hands. Rogers assured Dingell that he had done all he could do and that the automobile industry would respond with new technology to meet emission requirements. He lauded Dingell for not trying to stop the bill. Before long, they were friends again.

Strict automobile-emission standards were included in the conference agreement; shortly thereafter, President Carter signed the Clean Air Act Amendments. It was hailed as the most far-reaching environmental law ever passed. Rogers gave credit to each of the many factions he had cobbled together and to his many allies in the Congress.

One of the important results of the battle was the trust Rogers engendered in the Watergate class, especially among those on the Commerce Committee. He might be a conservative or, at best, a moderate, but he was making changes. That's what they had come to Washington to do. They could trust him and follow him.*

THE NATIONAL CANCER ACT

Of all the legislation he produced, the National Cancer Act, 1971 probably best reflects Rogers' mastery of the legislative process and the esteem in which his colleagues held him.

The Senate version of the National Cancer Act, passed with only one dissenting vote, would have effectively separated the National Cancer Institute from the National Institutes of Health. Rogers chose not to rubber-stamp the measure. Had he done so, the House would have quickly enacted the Senate version. He did not agree with the basic thrust of the bill, that taking NCI out of NIH was the most effective way to mount a national campaign against cancer. He believed that such a move would only hamper the effort, do harm to nearly all other biomedical research, and lead to the dismantling of NIH.

---

* With the Administration and Congress prepared to review Federal curbs on pollution in early 2005, the *Washington Post* ran a story on a 1990 EPA study concluding "that if the government had not acted [in 1970], 205,000 more Americans would have died early and millions more would have suffered from heart disease, chronic bronchitis, asthma, and other respiratory illnesses" in the first two decades after the law was passed. In addition, the act saved the nation between $6 trillion and $50 trillion in health costs and $523 billion from productivity not lost.[1]

When he announced there would be hearings, he knowingly set sail against a mighty wind and stayed the course.

The Senate bill was sponsored by Ted Kennedy (D-Mass.). Supporters included the American Cancer Society, a roster of noted medical professionals, influential Wall Street figures with White House connections, and syndicated columnist Ann Landers. The mastermind was Mary Lasker. She was a wealthy New York widow with a reputation for championing health causes, including years of lobbying Congress for more NIH funding. Lasker was also an honorary chair of the American Cancer Society and a member of the National Cancer Institute Advisory Council. She knew her way around Washington.

Using her vast network of friends, she persuaded Ralph Yarborough (D-Tex.), chairman of the Senate health committee, to establish a special panel, the National Panel of Consultants on the Conquest of Cancer. The panel was headed and populated by Mrs. Lasker's friends. Benno Schmidt, a lawyer who later became a managing partner in the J. H. Whitney & Co. investment firm, was a co-chair. Before coming to Wall Street, Schmidt had attended the University of Texas School of Law where he studied under Yarborough. Schmidt was also a major contributor to Republican candidates. Elmer Bobst, an elderly, but active man who had made millions in the pharmaceutical industry, also served on the cancer panel. Bobst had one singular distinction—he was known as Nixon's "honorary father."* It was Bobst who outlined the upside of the proposed Senate bill to Nixon, persuading him to become involved in the issue.

The panel of consultants reported that the NIH bureaucracy was a burden, slowing the work of the National Cancer Institute. NCI's research was producing promising leads, but there was not enough money to pursue

* At the 1995 dedication of the Nixon Center for Peace and Freedom (housed in the Elmer and Mamdouha Bobst Building in Washington, D.C.), Tricia Nixon Cox commented on Bobst's special relationship with the Nixons, saying that Bobst was "an extraordinary person whose life personified the idea of being dedicated to worthy causes . . . a self-made man whose intelligence, character, loyalty, patriotism, courage and generosity in many areas . . . made him an embodiment of the American dream. A mentor and father-figure to my father in all seasons since 1953, Elmer Bobst, or Uncle Elmer as Julie and I called him, was also a singular friend who, with his wife Mamdouha, shared my father's vision of a more just and peaceful world."

them. There was insufficient emphasis on applied research at NIH; instead the cancer institute was waiting for breakout cures from basic or bench research. The nation should launch a war on cancer by creating a focused, NASA-like program. The NCI director should report directly to the President. Ergo, the government's cancer entity should be a separate authority apart from the National Institutes of Health.

On its face, this proposition was appealing. The NASA allusion soon led to the familiar refrain, "If we can send a man to the moon, why can't we cure cancer by applying the same template." An Ann Landers column, calling on readers to support the Senate bill, brought in tens of thousands of pieces of mail to the Senate. Republican Alan Cranston, the senior senator from California, reportedly received more than 60,000 postcards. The President, responding to Bobst's urging, used his State of the Union address to announce he would budget an additional $100 million for cancer research.

It takes 218 votes to pass a bill in the House. More than 270 legislators had introduced the Senate bill in the House to show their support for a new cancer research organization. Rogers announced he would hold hearings on the bill, and he decided to build a case for a better way to fight cancer. Other committee chairs might place little value on protracted hearings, but unlike them, Rogers believed in building a solid record. He always gave all stakeholders an opportunity to present their views. In this case, comprehensive hearings would slow the push toward separation and give him time to educate members of Congress and the public.

For three weeks, Rogers heard from an array of scientists, researchers, administrators, and medical professionals. In all, 51 witnesses—representing a virtual who's who of biomedical research—testified, matched by an equal number of advocates from the public. Privately, Dr. Michael DeBakey, heart surgeon, head of Baylor Medical School and virtually an American idol for his work on the heart-lung machine, told Rogers that if cancer was split out from NIH, the American Heart Association would move for independence for the Heart and Lung Institute, too. Cancer may be the most-feared disease, but more people died of heart disease.

Three groups in particular added great weight to Rogers' position: the Association of American Medical Colleges, the American Medical Association, and the Foundation of American Societies for Experimental

Biology. Then David Baltimore, a researcher working under an NIH grant at the Massachusetts Institute of Technology, provided the bill's silver bullet. He had recently presented a groundbreaking report on the role virus enzymes play in causing cancer.

Rogers: You received support from the NIH leading to your discovery?

Baltimore: Yes, I did.

Rogers: From the National Cancer Institute?

Baltimore: No. From the National Institute on Allergy and Infectious Diseases.

Baltimore received a Nobel Prize for this work. Joined by other researchers, he made the point that no one knows where the answers to cancer will come from, but the interaction of the various NIH institutes strengthens the possibility of major discoveries.

Rogers was ready to accept most of the provisions in the Senate bill, except for the separation portion. In response to the cancer panel's complaint about grants slowed down by paperwork, he inserted language to fast-track grants. He provided for the NCI director to send the institutes' budget directly to the President. He reinstituted a cancer control program that Nixon had zeroed out in the previous budget. Up to now, the cancer institute had been first among equals. Rogers would give it a special standing.

To pressure subcommittee members into accepting the Senate bill, an ad hoc group called the Citizens Committee for the Conquest of Cancer, led by Dr. Solomon Garb of the Children's Hospital in Denver, and the American Cancer Society placed $56,000 worth of ads in the *Washington Post* and the hometown newspapers of 13 subcommittee members. The ads said that Congress, specifically the House subcommittee, was holding up the fight against cancer by not accepting the Senate bill, which had only one vote against it. But the members of the health committee resented this heavy-handed approach, and the ads had the opposite effect. The subcommittee and the full Commerce Committee went with Rogers.

KNOW THEM BY THE HOURS THEY KEEP

One night Rogers' staffer Bob Maher entered an elevator in the Capitol, with a stack of papers under one arm to be read by the congressman, two stops up. As the door closed, the operator asked, "You work for Congressman Rogers?" Maher replied, "Yes, how'd you know?" The operator answered, "Rogers' staff works all the time."

Rogers had used the hearing process to demonstrate the potential harm of removing NCI from NIH not only to cancer research, but also to the other institutes and their constituencies. The professional groups supporting him had strong scientific credentials, and he urged them to speak out on behalf of the House bill in meetings with committee members, through letters, and in op-ed pieces. He answered any question a House member had about his position, and he sent cogent explanations to his peers to counter surges from supporters of the Senate bill, always careful not to promise a cure for cancer. Instead he presented a case for biomedical research. The House overwhelmingly agreed, 350 to 5.

In the final days of November 1971, House and Senate conferees met at the Capitol to reconcile the differences in their bills. Rogers and Kennedy, both freshman chairmen, were honor-bound to hold on to the provisos that their chambers had each endorsed overwhelmingly. Their personalities and friendship soon took the edge off the stern positioning that usually takes place in the early phases of such conferences. Each saw the merit in certain provisions of the other's bill.

President Nixon had first resisted separation, later agreeing to bring the NCI director into the White House with a separate budget. Just before the House-Senate conference, he let it be known that he would support the House position. At one point in the discussion, Kennedy said to Rogers, invoking Nixon's name, "Why don't we ask the President to tell us which provision he prefers? And we can abide by that."

Rogers looked up and smiled. "I want this on the record: Kennedy asking President Nixon for advice and agreeing to abide by it." Everyone burst into laughter, Kennedy included. Any tension that had been building up quickly dissipated. And the revised agreed-on National Cancer Act went to the White House. President Nixon signed the bill into law on December 21, 1971. He later declared that it was the most important piece of legislation that ever crossed his desk.

New citizen, Paul Grant Rogers, born June 4, 1921.

Florence Roberts Rogers, undated. Paul's mother expected her sons "to always do the right thing." Warm and outgoing, very social, she entertained frequently, and definitely did not believe in paper napkins! Paul favors his mother in looks; his brothers take more after his father.

Dwight Laing Rogers Sr., 1950, after two terms in Congress. Paul's father, born, raised, and educated in Georgia, moved his law practice from Georgia to Florida in 1925, during the boom days. The boom went bust soon after. Becky and Paul's daughter, Laing, carries his middle name.

A toddler in Georgia. Even at this early age, the small Paul was already beginning to look like the adult Paul.

Teenager Paul in the typical Florida golfing garb of the day.

Second Lieutenant Paul Rogers, 1942. At Fort Bragg, North Carolina, the soldiers could ride the horses for recreation before assignment overseas.

Congressman Dwight Laing Rogers Sr. (D-Fla.), with his sons, early 1950s. His three boys followed him into the legal profession; Paul followed him all the way to Capitol Hill. From left, Dwight Jr., Dwight Sr., Doyle, and Paul. Today, Dwight Jr. is a lawyer and banker; Doyle is a lawyer and civic leader.

Seatmates Jackie Kennedy and Paul Rogers, passengers on what was probably a private plane, late 1961 or 1962. With a residence in Palm Beach, President Kennedy would periodically offer his neighbor a plane ride home to Florida. Shortly after John Glenn's historic space flight, the Kennedy's invited the original seven astronauts for a weekend in Florida. Paul was standing by when Jackie introduced Caroline to the "man who has flown all the way around the globe." The child looked at Glenn and piped up, "But where's the monkey?"

President John Kennedy and Paul Rogers at the Palm Beach Airport, early 1962. John Kennedy was campaigning in Florida for Rogers at the time.

Paul and Becky Rogers' engagement picture, West Palm Beach, December 1, 1962. The couple married two weeks later, and honeymooned in New Orleans and Palm Beach.

Rebecca Bell's wedding announcement photo, 1962. She keeps her wedding photos in a book, not good enough to show.

Laing, 5 months old, with parents, April 1964. There were so many pictures of her around the house, visitors could be overheard murmuring, "But I thought they had only one child."

To Becky Rogers –
with best wishes,
Lyndon B. Johnson

Lyndon Johnson, then vice president, twirling a pregnant Becky Rogers around the dance floor, 1963, at his vice presidential residence, before there was an official vice president's house. This one had previously belonged to legendary hostess Perle Mesta.

Becky Rogers, one of three congressional wives modeling Paris fashions at the French Embassy, May 1963. The beneficiary was the Seton Guild. About this time, national columnist Art Buchwald named her one of the ten most beautiful women in Washington.

Congressmen John Dingell and Paul Rogers had much in common, including their daughters, Spring 1964. Here, Dingell holds his daughter, nicknamed Dooley, and Rogers holds Laing.

President Kennedy signs the Mental Retardation Facilities and Community Mental Health Centers Construction Act, October 3, 1963. From left, Senator George Smathers (D-Fla.), Paul Rogers, and President Kennedy. The legislation, opening the way to care and living facilities within the community, as well as more research, was the last bill Kennedy signed into law.

President Johnson taking a break from a cabinet meeting to greet some official visitors, Spring 1967. Presidential Assistant Jack Valenti had arranged for a few children to meet the President. Foreground, from left, Valenti, Angela Wisal, Laing Rogers invited by Johnson to join the group, Billy Watson, President Johnson, Michael Dickerson, Courtenay Valentine. In the background from left, Secretary of State Dean Rusk, Undersecretary of State George Ball, Mrs. Marvin Watson, wife of the postmaster general, and Secretary of Defense Robert McNamara.

Coming to consensus, 1970. Senate-House conferees mark up the National Diabetes Mellitus Research and Education Act. Sen. Richard Schweiker sits left front; next to him is Sen. Ted Kennedy. Right front is House Commerce Committee chairman, Harley Staggers, with health subcommittee member Paul Rogers just behind.

A close end game: Who will gain control of the healthcare chessboard, 1977. The collage was a gift to Rogers from NIH Director Don Frederickson. Note: In the Senate, Ted Kennedy was responsible for healthcare legislation, Muskie (like Kennedy, a presidential aspirant) handled environmental matters. In the House, Rogers did both.

Well-wishers gather around Tip O'Neill just sworn in as Speaker of the House, January 1977. He gave his first autograph as Speaker to Laing, standing at the left next to her dad.

Examining the plaques at the March 16, 1973, dedication of the Paul G. Rogers Federal Building and U.S. Courthouse in West Palm Beach, Florida. From left, Paul's mother, Mrs. Dwight Laing Rogers, Sr.; Paul Rogers; daughter Laing Sisto; and Becky Rogers.

The White House signing that almost wasn't, December 23, 1971. Paul Rogers and Ted Kennedy, co-sponsors of the National Cancer Act, join President Nixon at the Presidential signing. Nixon had opposed a formal White House ceremony because it meant that Kennedy would be there. Fearful that the young senator was going to run against him for the Presidency, he did not want to give his possible opponent any publicity. Nixon relented only after Mary Lasker, the doyenne of biomedical research, called Elmer Bobst, Nixon's close friend, who convinced the President of the politic thing to do.

Paul Rogers and President Ford, 1988. The two men met to discuss health matters.

The four winners of the 1993 Albert Lasker Award with benefactor Mary Lasker (seated) and some of the prestigious guests at the awards ceremony in New York City. From left, Dr. Donald Metcalf, who won the award for medical research; Dr. Nancy Wexler and the Hon. Paul Rogers, who each received public service awards; Hillary Clinton, speaker; Dr. Gunther Blobel, medical research award winner; and Dr. Jordan Gutterman, chairman of the Awards Committee. The Lasker Award is the most prestigious U.S. honor for work in the health-sciences. One-half of the winners, like Dr. Blobel, have gone on to become Nobel winners.

A Rose Garden happening, December 12, 1977. Jimmy Carter signing the Medicare-Medicaid Anti-Fraud and Abuse Amendments. Those attending, from left, Congressmen Doug Walgren (Penn.), Bill Brodhead (Mich.), Henry Waxman (Calif.), Jim Floria (N.J.), Senator Herman Talmadge (Ga.), Paul Rogers, President Carter at the table, Congressmen Tim Lee Carter (Ky.), Charles Vanik (D-Ohio), HHS Secretary Joe Califano, Congressmen Dan Rostenkowski (Ill.), Jim Scheuer (N.Y.), Harley Staggers (W. Va.), and Richardson Preyer (N.C.).

Framed displays lining a wall in the Rogers' home, Washington, D.C., 2004. The images showcase many—but not all—of the congressman's legislative victories. "This is what we could fit on the wall," comments Becky Rogers.

THE WHITE HOUSE

WASHINGTON

6-23-78

To Congressman Paul Rogers

Your resigning from the Congress will be a great loss for our nation.

I wish you had asked for my permission to do this. I would have refused.

Your friend

Jimmy Carter

Father and daughter in the congressman's office, June 1967. Taken by a Capitol photographer for Father's Day, the picture appeared in Sunday newspapers across the country on the holiday.

Becky and Paul Rogers, 1988, snapped by a photographer as they stepped out of a hotel in Newport, Rhode Island, where Paul was attending a conference.

The brothers take their mother out for a 102nd birthday lunch celebration at the Yacht Club, Ft. Lauderdale, March 9, 1992. A widow for 39 years, she died at age 104.

One happy guy! Montana 1980. Fly-fishing is Paul's favorite recreation.

Paul Rogers, June 12, 2002. At a ceremony celebrating the Congressionally-directed naming of the Paul Grant Rogers Plaza on the grounds of NIH, Paul declared, "Without research there is no hope! No hope for diagnosis, for treatment, or to cure diseases. Research brings hope and better health to our nation."

Three generations of the Rogers family vacationing at a dude ranch in Jackson Hole, Wyoming, Summer 2001. Atop the fence, from left, the Sisto's: Cole, 9; Laing; Rebecca, 4; Lily, 6; Alexandra, 11; and John. In front, Becky and Paul Rogers.

Chapter 4

Moving On

When Jimmy Carter was elected president in 1976, the press poked fun at all manner of traditions and quirks of the South. The humor ranged from warm to bitter. Before him, Lyndon Johnson, a longtime fixture in Washington, could not escape the pundits. Would there be pickup trucks on the lawn of the White House? Would grits be served at state dinners? Even Paul Rogers' hometown paper, the *Palm Beach Post*, rushed to print a hilarious softcover book, *How to Speak Southern*, to serve as a Rosetta Stone for the rest of the nation.

Actually, Rogers' speech never had the cadence or the colloquialisms of the Deep South. However, he did have a southerner's way of blurring the difference between a statement, a question, and an order.

For example, if a visiting luminary was in town, Rogers might tell you, "I was thinking about dinner with Jim Smith." It was to be understood from this statement that he was asking you to join them. So it was unusual when Bette Ann Starkey, the keeper of Congressman Rogers' calendar, actually transmitted an order one day in mid-1978: "The Boss wants you to go to dinner tonight."

Later in the day, she passed on the only detail—the setting for the meeting, a little-known restaurant in a quiet little-known hotel. Near the appointed hour, four staffers slipped, one by one, into the restaurant.

Rogers held court, sipping a drink before dinner. Soon, he drew himself up straight abruptly. "It's getting to the time when I have to decide whether to stand for re-election."

THE STRANGE CASE OF L'ORANGE MAROC

Congressman Rogers liked to be nice to his staff. One day, in San Francisco for a committee hearing, he learned of a highly touted French restaurant and called ahead to make reservations for his group. When the congressman and staff arrived, right on time, Rogers asked for his table, but they found themselves waiting inordinately long before being seated. From then on, things went from bad to worse, from poor food to inattentive service.

The congressman from Florida struck back. After the waiter recited the evening's roster of desserts, Rogers ordered L'Orange Maroc for all! It was not on the dessert list. The waiter checked with the kitchen, only to return with the dismaying news, "We have never heard of L'Orange Maroc, sir." Rogers asked for the maître d'.

Embarassed, the maître d' confirmed that there was no knowledge of L'Orange Maroc anywhere in the restaurant. "Why not make it!" suggested the congressman. And to make sure the kitchen would put the dessert together correctly, he passed on his expert advice, demonstrating how a whole orange per person must be carefully sliced into thin circular discs, topped with some Grand Marnier, and then sprinkled with freshly grated cinnamon.

A little while later, the maître d' returned. "We don't have any grated cinnamon, sir. We only have sticks of it!" Said Rogers, "Then, use a grater and grate it!"

And so the Rogers staff enjoyed what seemed to be a great new French dessert made wholly from the cloth of their boss's imagination. Actually, he later told them, he had recalled the ingredients of a dessert at a Moroccan Embassy dinner.

Smiles, even laughter, broke out. Surely, he was kidding. Rogers usually ran against only token opposition. In his last campaign he had garnered 92 percent of the vote, one of the highest margins in any House race. Furthermore, there had not been even a whisper about a Republican challenger. In all probability, he was at a point where he might never be seriously challenged at the ballot. What was up? At age 57, Rogers was a man in his prime, respected and revered. He enjoyed his work and did it exceedingly

GOING MY WAY?

I remember how Rogers would put his arm around you and then put his hand on your arm and lead you down the hall. Before you know it, you're talking with him, and you're heading in his direction and discussing his program.

—Professional staffer Jeff Schwartz

well. "I'm serious," Rogers continued soberly. "We should let possible candidates know whether or not I'm going to run again."

He continued, "We have accomplished a lot. There is not a lot left to be done, other than national health insurance. And I don't really see a national health insurance plan anywhere in the near future. I think it's going to be harder and harder to get action on the environment. The Clean Air Act Amendments took two years of work, and it's going to take some time for that to get settled out. There might even be a backlash. We've done well on the health side, but I think the pendulum is going to start swinging the other way. It will be a while before we can get much more done on new initiatives."

"Also, this is Laing's last year in high school. You know I haven't spent enough time with her, and I want to be around for this last year before she heads off to college."

Then he looked to the future. "It would be one thing if I had a reasonable chance to be chairman of the Commerce Committee, but Harley Staggers and John Dingell will be there as long as they want the job."

"After all, I'm at an age where, if I ever want to do something other than be in Congress, it's time to get started. I'm on pretty good terms with the President and he has two more years. That might help in whatever I might end up doing. I just don't want to be a lobbyist."

When Rogers retired, some of his staff went back to Florida but most joined law firms, trade associations, and consulting firms in Washington. Rogers' top staffer in his district office, Dan Mica, ran for his boss's seat, and won.

PART II

The Hogan & Hartson Years

Former Iowa Governor Bob Ray and Paul Rogers, as co-chairs of the National Coalition for Health Care, meeting with Hillary Clinton, 1993. The First Lady was about to address an NCHC meeting. The organization has been working for universal health care since 1986.

Chapter 5

Paul Rogers, Private Citizen

Congressman Paul Rogers morphed seamlessly from his role as a rainmaker for health, environment, and science policy on Capitol Hill into a successful lawyer at Hogan & Hartson, a 100-year-old law practice, based in Washington, D.C. At Hogan & Hartson, he capitalized on the credibility he had earned in the House of Representatives, continuing to provide solutions to complex health and medical issues, including how to get policy accomplished. His experience in Congress, his skill at bringing together divergent views, and his understanding of where the other side was coming from attracted new clients to the firm. He helped the firm develop a premier health-law section. Ever the champion of the nation's health, Rogers also undertook pro bono work.

The only perturbation he recalls came in his beginning days at Hogan & Hartson. A Food and Drug Administration official dropped by to invite him to a meeting. "When she called me 'Paul,' I realized that I was now playing in a different ballpark." He may still have been Mr. Health, but he was no longer Mr. Rogers to the government or his co-workers. He adjusted well.

Ann Vickery, head of the health-law practice and office managing partner, calls Rogers' role in building the practice "unique and essential."

> Paul has been and continues to be the role model who keeps us all striving to be better at what we do. Many of us who would have drifted off into other lives have stayed the course because we see so clearly that he has made an enormous contribution to the common good while also serving as a trusted advisor to paying clients.

Today, the Hogan & Hartson health practice comprises more than 40 health lawyers helping clients across all segments of the health industry deal with challenging legislative and regulatory problems. They work on project teams with transaction, litigation, and intellectual property specialists to change laws and regulations, close deals, and win cases. They prosecute patents for academic health centers and other health providers; for pharmaceutical, medical device, and biotechnology companies; for trade associations and medical specialty societies; and for clients whose business involves healthcare. In addition, the firm has been able to attract other public servants, "in large part, because Paul Rogers is here," says Vickery.

FROM ONE WHO KNOWS!

Comments Paul G. Dembling, a former general counsel for the U.S. Government Accounting Office and the National Aeronautics and Space Agency, who dealt with Congressman Rogers over the years: "I always liked Congressman Rogers. One, he's got the same two first initials that I have [P.G.]. And, two, he's the only politician I know who doesn't act like one."

Rogers appears a number of times in a book commissioned by Hogan & Hartson to commemorate its 100th anniversary. In 1981, only a few years after Paul joined Hogan & Hartson, a group of hospice leaders visited him. They thought Medicare coverage should apply to hospice services just as it does to hospitals and nursing homes. Could Rogers help? Rogers let his visitors know that the firm would help them as much as possible.

But he also knew there was trouble ahead. Ronald Reagan had just been elected President on a platform of reducing the Federal government and the taxes that supported it. Any growth in programs like Medicare was nigh unthinkable in the new political atmosphere of rebellion against government spending and "entitlement" programs. After the hospice owners

> **RESPECT FOR ALL**
>
> Here was Paul Grant Rogers—the embodiment of what people thought a congressman should look like—impeccable dress, custom shirts, gold cufflinks (the male staff emulated him and also dressed that way), great orator, getting famous as a subcommittee chair—and he treated the shoe-shine guy, waiters, and elevator operators in the Capitol no differently than he treated his colleagues in Congress. He remembered their names, knew something about them, asked how they were doing, and always shook their hands. —Chief counsel Steve Lawton

left, Rogers called in Vickery and Earl (Duke) Collier [formerly the Deputy Administrator for the Health and Human Services Health Care Financing Administration] and asked their advice. Vickery recalls what they both recommended: "Pray."

For the next year and a half, Vickery said, she, Rogers, and Collier became "zealots" on behalf of their hospice clients, who also worked vigorously for their cause. At last, in 1982, Congress surprised everyone by passing legislation allowing Medicare benefits for hospice care. It was the only expansion of Medicare benefits of any kind passed by Congress that year, and it was the turning point in Vickery's career. "I've been a health lawyer ever since," she says. "That was my introduction, and it stuck." The National Hospice and Palliative Care [Organization] stuck with Hogan & Hartson, too, and has remained a client ever since.

Another anecdote involves a pro bono project undertaken almost a decade later on behalf of the Grand Canyon Trust. The firm was helping the trust convince the Environmental Protection Agency to do something about pollution in the nation's first national park. Rogers had questioned EPA witnesses sharply about Grand Canyon pollution during hearings leading up to the passage of the Clean Air Act Amendments of 1977. The tables were now turned.

> Rogers was the first witness at the March 18, 1991, hearings in Phoenix. He testified that in 1977 the EPA had promised his committee that it would retrofit the Navajo generating station with "scrubbers" to reduce sulfur dioxide emissions. Borrowing Iraqi leader Saddam Hussein's widely parodied reference to the 1990–1991 Gulf War as "the mother of all battles," Rogers called the power plant "the mother of all pollution" in the Grand Canyon.

IT'S ALL RELATIVE, PART 2

Becky Rogers remembers: "After graduating from college, our daughter Laing thought she might enter the field of fashion. One of the stops on her career path was an internship at Macy's Department Store in New York City. About a week into the job, while involved in a stint as a saleswoman, the supervisor called her aside to explain, 'You don't have to be *that* nice to the customers, Laing.' "

It was a perfect "sound bite" for the news media, which gave the hearing national coverage. Rogers' testimony, along with a videotape of sulfur dioxide vapors wafting down the canyon and computer-generated slides illustrating reduced visibility, formed a compelling indictment of the power plant's environmental performance.

Hogan & Hartson proceeded to craft a compromise plan that resulted in a settlement signed with much fanfare by President George H.W. Bush at the Grand Canyon. More than 20 years after the initial enactment of the first Clean Air Act, Paul Rogers was still on top of the issue.

Chapter 6

The Path Audit of Medicare Changes

Paul Rogers got involved in a crisis of nationwide import in the mid-1990s when the inspector general at the Department of Health and Human Services announced a nationwide audit, in conjunction with the Department of Justice, of major teaching hospitals and their faculty-billing practices. In so doing, Rogers helped the nation's health sciences schools and teaching hospitals respond to the proposed retrospective path audit announced by the two departments, and he helped to preserve the fiscal stability of many of these institutions.

Over the decades since the establishment of Medicare in 1965, guidelines, rules, and regulations had been written and rewritten to govern which physician services the Federal government will reimburse and how these services are to be formally documented. Concurrently, various regional Medicare officials, while attempting to adhere to whatever set of rules and regulations governing faculty clinical compensation was currently in use, interpreted these regulations differently. This situation had created great ambiguity among the players as to what constituted proper adherence to government rules and regulations.

When the nationwide audit began, it utilized rules and regulations published after the period being audited, applying them retroactively. Six audits were already underway when news came of a settlement by the

University of Pennsylvania in excess of $30 million for infractions plus a three-fold penalty. It was Rogers' guidance that helped the health sciences community unite to fight the proposed audit publicly.

In brief—and without trying to bring the uninitiated into the arcane world of Medicare physician-billing requirements vis-à-vis academic health centers—Medicare pays to the teaching hospital a sum for the salaries and teaching costs of residents (post-MD and DDS graduate students). This amount is calculated on the basis of a formula that perhaps no one understands, but that is connected to the number of residents at the hospital. From Medicare's point of view, both the service and teaching costs of the resident staff are thereby recompensed.

Faculty physicians may also bill Medicare for clinical services they personally render. The faculty member who, for example, performs a cardiac catheterization or removes a malignant melanoma, must verify taking part in the billable event. If an audit were to reveal that, on the date of the billed and recompensed service, the faculty member was actually out of town, the payment would have to be returned with interest, and a possible penalty three times the amount inappropriately collected by the hospital or the billing physician might also be inflicted.

In that audit of the University of Pennsylvania, the Inspector General's office had examined in depth 100 randomly selected Medicare patient records over the previous three-year period and the actual payments made by Medicare against the newest set of regulations. The amount charged in error in those charts was multiplied by the number of Medicare patients cared for at the university hospital (divided by 100). Medicare accepted the resulting estimate of overpayment as the total amount the university owed the agency, which could then also assess a triple penalty.

This came as a bombshell for the teaching-hospital community. Concerns heightened when word went out that the Department of Justice was threatening to level criminal charges against hospitals that had misstated their costs, especially if fraud was suspected. Soon after, the HHS-Inspector General came up with a new auditing proposal presenting two options. One would be for teaching hospitals to stand pat and await the IG audit, a stance presumably based on a degree of comfort with the process and how a hospital would fare. The other would be for an institution to conduct its own path audit under the same guidelines that the IG was using and thereby avoid a triple penalty if inappropriate payments surfaced. The options came with a deadline for selecting the preferred audit pathway.

To the teaching-hospital community the imposition of a deadline for the self-audit implied that the government was hoping that most institutions would conduct the audit themselves and conduct it promptly. The result would be a relatively quick return to Medicare of an estimated $1 billion in overpayments, plus interest (but with no fine).

Theoretically, the strategy of bringing the Department of Justice in up front, threatening clinicians and administrators with criminal charges, and gaining an initial "victory" in the University of Pennsylvania settlement, should have inclined the academic world to quickly begin the financially less painful, but more rapid, self-audits. A number of leaders at academic health centers, however, rejected this scenario, increasingly convinced that what they had once merely suspected was, in fact, the government strategy. Furthermore, many held that it was unfair to hold them to newly published standards for proof-of-service when assessing three-year-old records.

Politically, there seemed to be little sympathy for what some referred to as the "plight of the fat-cat specialist doctors," especially during a time of wide-ranging Medicare-fraud audits. Accordingly, some academic health center leaders, along with the senior staff of the Association of Academic Health Centers (AHC), saw no way to effectively resist the government's movement toward getting as much return as possible from teaching hospitals, even if it meant bringing institutions to their knees and regardless of what was actually right.

AHC asked Rogers, AHC's senior advisor, if he would be willing to get a Hogan & Hartson colleague, Republican Bob Michel from Illinois (who had served on the House Appropriations Committee), to a meeting on the issue. At the meeting with Rogers, Michel, and Bulger (author), the AHC president, were two AHC board members, Peter Kohler, president of the Oregon University of the Health Services, and Jerry Burrow, dean of the School of Medicine, Yale University. Also present were Jordan Cohen and Dick Knapp, president and senior vice president, respectively, of the Association of American Medical Colleges.

Rogers and Michel were asked to imagine that they were back in Congress as they listened to what teaching hospitals were going through, and then to offer advice on whether these institutions should go along with the self-administered audit or develop an active plan to counter the government's strategy.

For two hours, the advisors listened and asked difficult questions as they explored whether the issue really had substance or whether the AHC and AAMC representatives had been beset by the sky-is-falling mentality. Although expressing concern about the government's behavior (if, indeed, it could be verified), they withheld judgment. They said they would get in touch in a week. And they did.

The more Rogers' law firm, Hogan & Hartson, ran their traps, the more indignant Rogers became about the way the government's representatives were going about their business. He felt strongly that there was a way to achieve proper resolution without hammering the already fragile academic and hospital infrastructures that were so central to enhancing the nation's health status. Yet in this case, bureaucratic politics seemed to be the overriding concern.

Rogers, joined by Laura Loeb, a Hogan & Hartson associate, checked the law carefully and determined that the HHS-IG was applying the law retroactively. The result was that AHC and AAMC decided to fight the audit strategy and to do so publicly. Jointly, they hired Rogers to help guide and implement counterstrategies. AAMC also offered to provide a forum for the ongoing education of stakeholders by holding meetings demonstrating their control. They also brought in their own lawyers to help the two associations think through both legal and political courses of action.

With AAMC and AHC behind them, and with people who represented affected institutions meeting regularly, the teaching institutions were empowered to stay strong and fight for their cause, rather than succumb to the second audit pathway.

During one of AAMC's big strategy sessions, Rogers had not been asked to offer any comments. Neither had he been given a place on the program. Intent on winning for the teaching hospitals and their faculty, he positioned himself at the back of the center aisle, standing alone as a highly visible audience member. When the right time came, he made his point, taking over the meeting and subtly using his national stature to encourage continuing institutional resistance to bullying Federal officials. He may not have endeared himself to those who did not agree with him, but he did his job, coming across as someone to reckon with when health and science were threatened!

During this entire period, Rogers displayed other skills that one does not often come across in leaders, that is, the ability to muster popular resistance to an unjust situation and invoke the political force necessary for change. In the case of the path audit, he believed that by convincing powerful and appropriately placed people of the Medicare audit's questionable dimensions, effective warning signals would get directly to the HHS-IG. The inspector general, Rogers surmised, would then seek an amelioration of the more unsavory behaviors that people on the receiving end were complaining about.

And that is exactly what happened. Sixteen cases were dropped. Any strategy to transfer $1 billion in a year or two from the teaching hospitals to the Federal government was thwarted. Over the subsequent years, the number of institutions having to make sizable repayments constituted only a fraction of the universe. The total of all settlements was more in the range of $200 million than the government's expectation of $1 billion in "illegal billings" plus fines up to $3 for every dollar inappropriately billed.

During this period, Rogers and Loeb shared a willingness to listen and give counsel to those with a significant problem. They asked the hard questions and then collected the relevant data on their own.

Once the data were in hand, Rogers expressed what could be called "righteous indignation" regarding the overzealous behavior of the government agents. The magnitude of the financial threat to institutions essential to the nation's health and science efforts led him to an aggressive plan to forestall and counter the government's strategies. He was acting on a principle connected to the public good: he acted on what was right rather than acting as a lawyer who was protecting and defending his client, whatever the merits of the case in question.

Rogers commented once that he did not think Secretary Donna Shalala liked him very much. Perhaps the events unfolding around the path audit were the reason why.

Chapter 7

Growing the Nation's Biomedical Investment

Research!America (R!A) is a not-for-profit public education and advocacy group based in Alexandria, Virginia, dedicated to making government-sponsored medical and other health-related research a larger priority in the United States.*

Dr. William G. Anlyan, the first board chairman, recalls the early years of the organization.[1]

> Jack [Edmund] Whitehead, a former patient at Duke who at one point had considered putting his Whitehead Institute for Biomedical Research at Duke (it went to MIT), was concerned that when the era of Mary Lasker and her group had passed, it would leave a void in the public debate influencing health-related legislation, particularly as it concerns biomedical research support, in Washington. [Mary Lasker was a well-connected private citizen with

* When it was launched in January 1989, the Research!America alliance had about 100 members drawn from medical schools, pharmaceutical companies, voluntary health associations, and professional biomedical scientific societies. By 2004, it had expanded to 475 organization members, plus about 100 individual members who provide a much broader representation of academic health professional schools. A growing number of state and local organizations committed to research are also on board.

> a deep interest in medical research who had several powerful friends on congressional committees overseeing such legislation.] Whitehead founded Research!America in 1988, and was able to get former Senator Lowell Weicker (R-Conn.), who had been a champion of the NIH, as the full-time president of the new organization, headquartered in Alexandria, Virginia. Jack asked me to be on the board.
>
> Unfortunately, Senator Weicker, who had served as R!A CEO since 1987, a year before its formal launch, and who had insisted at the beginning that he was through with politics, saw the opportunity of running for the governorship of Connecticut. This led to a period of well over a year of indecision, with nothing moving until Weicker made up his mind. When he finally left in 1990 to run for governor, Jack Whitehead recruited Mary Woolley. She has been president of Research!America ever since.

Whitehead had hit a home run. Woolley had an active leadership background in biomedical research, serving first as administrator, then as chief executive officer, of the Medical Research Institute of San Francisco since 1981. She was not a nationally known figure and was largely unknown in political circles. But Whitehead must have recognized that Research!America needed a hands-on communicator and hard worker to help it realize its purpose.

One of the first things Woolley did was to introduce a public-survey instrument to yield new data about what people know and don't know about biomedical science, what scientific research they wanted, and what they would pay to support it.

After helping Woolley get acclimated and satisfying himself that she had the tools for moving R!A forward, Anlyan decided to turn the board chair over to someone else. He asked Ike (Roscoe) Robinson, his longtime friend and protégé who was then the vice chancellor for health affairs at Vanderbilt University, to head the search committee. Anlyan and Robinson quickly put Paul Rogers at the head of their list. But first they wanted to know just what he saw as R!A's future and how well Woolley and Rogers could form a new leadership in tandem. The issue was how dominant Rogers would want to be in his work with Woolley. That concern quickly vanished when it became clear that both were driven by mission rather than personal agenda.

Rogers' first reaction to Research!America's generous offer of yet another pro bono opportunity for him to serve the community was that the initial goal of sustaining the recent budgetary gains of the NIH was admirable enough, but it was essentially not enough to interest him in taking on the multiyear commitment as board chair. His response to the comeback question of the search committee, as to what goal would stir his interest, was simple: "To double the NIH budget in 5 years!"

Then, before he finally accepted, Rogers also wanted to know that his board agreed to a goal more ambitious than any R!A had ever had. He got that positive feedback when Robinson informed him of the results of the R!A leadership confab.

GOOD ENOUGH

Three year's ago I was called to Senator Frist's office to help draft anti-tobacco legislation. I met Senator Frist for the first time, and he asked me about my background. I said, "I'm with a law firm that represents the American Cancer Society." He said, "What else?" I said, "My firm does not take tobacco companies as clients." He said, "Go on." I said, "I used to work for Paul Rogers." Senator Frist said, "That's good enough for me. Get to work."

However, before finally accepting the chair, Rogers personally circled back to individuals to be certain they knew what a significant public opinion and political task lay before them and to gain their personal pledge to help him help R!A achieve something major for the added national investment in biomedical and related sciences. Recently, Rogers elaborated, saying, "Bill Anlyan had set the table for the organization that Jack Whitehead had the insight and vision to create, and I could see that Mary Woolley had the right values, motivation, and talents to take the next steps. All I needed to be certain of was the commitment of the board itself and other key research players."

Of course, Rogers and the board could not accomplish the job alone. But when Rogers said it could be done and needed to be done, or else the science community would stagnate politically, his view took hold among those who could make it happen. The credibility he had earned in the scientific, clinical research, and advocacy communities paid off once more.

A few months later, in January 1997, Research!America launched an aggressive two-pronged campaign: to bring the need for more biomedical research funding to the American public, and develop political venues that would take the public response seriously.

Under Rogers' insistent and constant encouragement, R!A members engaged in active outreach to bring in additional members, especially the politically powerful, disease-specific advocacy groups (e.g., those concerned with heart disease, cancer, diabetes, osteoporosis, neurological impairments) and profession-specific research groups (e.g., medicine, public health, dentistry, nursing, pharmacy, and allied health sciences). Educators and researchers from the universities, academic health centers, medical schools, and other major health professions came on board.*

The relevant associations (e.g., AHC, AAMC, American Association of Colleges of Pharmacy, American Dental Education Association, American Association of Colleges of Nursing, and Association of Schools of Public Health) also connected in various ways to what Rogers said, because they knew him either directly or by reputation, and did more than their share to promote membership in R!A and support the overall doubling effort.

Along the way, the heretofore single-silo, disease-advocacy groups like the American Cancer Society, the American Heart Association, and the Juvenile Diabetes Association had to be convinced that a rising tide in overall NIH support would lift all the boats. These voluntary health associations are vitally important to the cause of research in terms of public and political advocacy. Paul Rogers was the central force in bringing these groups together in a common purpose.

Meanwhile, the initial national R!A surveys evolved into studies of public attitudes toward biomedical research and the related sciences at the

* The energy of leaders—like Bill Peck, recently retired vice president for medical affairs at Washington University; Columbia University physiology professor Dr. Samuel Silverstein, who serves part-time at the Lasker/Funding First Program; Bill Brinkley, a world-class educator from Baylor University; and, more recently, Dr. Jay Gershen, former dean of dentistry at the University of California at Los Angeles and currently executive vice chancellor at the University of Colorado—brought about a phenomenal growth in new members.

state level as well as repeatable national surveys whose results could be compared year to year. Focus-group results also added to the general knowledge base, revealing some of the rationale behind public attitudes. The political significance of gathering area-specific, public-opinion data was clear to Rogers, if not to all R!A members at first. Legislators and appointed officials at the state, regional, and local levels are naturally interested in polling data that reveal the attitudes and priorities of their constituents. The same held true for their media counterparts.

Thus, under Rogers' aegis, all R!A efforts to double the NIH budget were informed by a continuing flow of data from local, state, and national polls on how America feels about healthcare and the role of biomedical research in maintaining and enhancing health. The findings, in turn, became the focus of widespread communication, careful planning, collaborative thinking, and action.

In his first speech to the R!A membership in 1996, Rogers had introduced the concept of extending the public-opinion surveys into each of the nation's 435 congressional districts and then taking the results to both the influential people and the rest of the populace in a district. 435 Project™ was born the following January with the aim to create a sustaining voice for research by engaging citizens across the country as advocates for medical and health research. The immediate strategy was to bring the R!A message on the importance of medical and health research to the nation and on its corollary—the need to double the NIH budget over a five-year period—to five primary audiences in each district: the media, elected officials, the general public, community leaders, and the scientific community.

Relying on his carefully crafted coalition building, Rogers enlisted former Senator Paul Simon (D-Ill.), and Louis Sullivan, MD, former HHS Secretary under President George H. W. Bush, to head the project's national leadership council. Rogers recruited other outstanding people to the cause. Together, Rogers and Woolley secured initial funding support from the Burroughs Welcome Fund, the Charles A. Dana Foundation, the Robert Wood Johnson Foundation, the Mary Woodard Lasker Charitable Trust, the Lucille P. Mackey Foundation, the Donald W. Reynolds Foundation, and the Whitehead Charitable Foundation. As success bred success, many more supporters started to come forward.

People recruited to participate in 435 Project™ activities were encouraged to clarify the many ways in which biomedical and related research serves the public interest not only in the nation and the world at large, but also in their hometowns.

R!A tailored messages, whether for delivery in public forums or through print ads and sound bites to the specific concerns of the targeted community, from public health to employment.

Too often researchers and advocates for research do not take into account the importance of speaking to their various publics, or they have little experience or comfort with doing so. 435 Project™ makes the job easier by holding special R!A workshops locally. In addition, advocates also have access to R!A white papers on where the healthcare dollar goes; sample op-ed pieces and letters to the editor; and disease-specific one-pagers describing how biomedical research saves lives and money.

Through activities like calling on editorial boards and television and radio producers; speaking to church, school, and civic groups; and visiting the local offices of elected officials, 435 Project™ participants have elevated the importance of medical and health-related research in general and, more specifically, the significance of giving a jump start to American biomedical science by doubling the NIH budget over five years. By engaging in such dialogues, they not only put a human face (namely, their own) on research, but also make friends for research by bringing its benefits closer to home.

As the project progressed, more and more researchers became comfortable connecting with their elected representatives. Among the early success stories is the visit by Steve Hyman, MD, director of the National Institute of Mental Health, and R!A board member John Whitehead to Republican Speaker Dennis Hastert's Illinois district. Meeting with NIH-funded researchers at Northern Illinois University and members of the academic and broader community, including patient advocates, Hyman and Whitehead made the connection between the work of a large Federal agency, the outstanding research being conducted in their community, and the strong approval of Hastert's constituents for medical research.

Elsewhere, project activities propelled local citizens into action. When Colorado became the site for R!A statewide surveys, local citizens brought the survey results to important elected representatives. Senator

Ben Nighthorse Campbell (R-Colo.), upon learning that the vast majority of his constituents favored increased research monies even if it meant increased taxes and that a similar majority did not know where the senator stood on the issue, immediately called a press conference to proclaim his support for increased NIH research dollars.

Don Capra, chief executive officer of the Oklahoma Medical Research Foundation, became an advocate for more research funding and started to write a weekly column on medical research for the local press. Other Oklahoma citizens started visiting local editorial boards regularly, and many developed informal speakers bureaus to facilitate outreach to civic and church groups. Patient advocates and other volunteers distributed thousands of brochures, bumper stickers, and other collateral materials extolling the value of medical research.

A SIMPLE CONCEPT

French-born Micheline Lange, Rogers' secretary at Hogan & Hartson, uses the French word "simple" to describe the consistency and constancy of her boss's character and personal behavior.

"In French," she explains, "*simple* means to be the same through and through. What you see is what you get no matter how thinly you slice the cheese."

In Kentucky, the city of Lexington developed an annual Research!Lexington program, bringing together researchers, media, students, and other members of the community to discuss the state of health research in their city.

The push to develop political advocacy venues led to a new effort by Hogan & Hartson. The law firm set up a not-for-profit, biomedical-research advocacy entity led by Whitehead's son John, who remains involved with the Whitehead Institute and other health causes. The group mobilized the legislative and government relations arms of various research-oriented organizations, universities, the health and disease-specific community, and corporations around the doubling effort.

By January 2003, the United States Congress had appropriated the fifth-year funds needed to bring the FY 1998 budget of $13.6 billion to

$27.2 billion. Together, Paul Rogers and Bob Michel had spent more than 300 hours visiting senators and representatives and educating them about the need for a greater Federal investment in NIH. Their leadership by example did not go unnoticed in the scientific community, transforming Research!America from a nascent, little-known, not-for-profit organization into a highly influential instrument for change in many parts of the nation.

Research!America is now applying the 435 Project™* concept to all of its public outreach activities, identifying key districts for intensified activity on a year-to-year basis depending on the national legislative and regulatory agenda for medical and health research and research policy. Thus, the compelling vision of the project, and indeed of Research!America—to inspire and empower advocates for biomedical research all across the nation—has been writ large.

Observes Mary Woolley, "When I work with Paul, I come away feeling I want somehow to become a better person! . . . At the very least, you feel better working in common with him toward a tangible goal."

What talents and other resources did Paul Rogers bring to the effort? First and foremost, he had a vision: to dramatically expand the size, scope, and reach of biomedical research in the United States. For him, the hope that comes with today's research is a core belief, not a political spin. Hope is not something health economists try to measure, which then gets neglected or discounted in the social calculus of experts. Instead, Rogers declares, hope springs from a reasonable, accountable social investment in research that sustains and nourishes our nation and, indeed, the world.

Additionally, his coalition-building skills, his hands-on, inclusive leadership style, his respect for others, and his capacity to listen furthered achievement of the goals that make up that vision. And when the goals were reached, Rogers gave (and continues to give) the credit for success to

---

* An early component of what became the 435 Project™ was a Mail-to-the-Chief computerized letter-writing campaign for reaching the President and Congress, made available at annual meetings of professional and voluntary health societies. The current equivalent is a grassroots-activism tool, ADS Tech's CapWiz, an inexpensive, commercial software package that includes a video-capture capability on politically pressing issues and a quick method for sending mail electronically.

others. This behavior has proved infectious, and it is a testimony to his leadership that so many others have adopted this practice.

Furthermore, he is not satisfied with just reaching a set goal. Instead, he raises the bar. While in the fourth year of the five-year doubling effort, Rogers began a discussion of accountability, declaring it incumbent on Research!America to translate through effective communications the billions of dollars of doubled NIH investment into societal and human benefits. Woolley and Rogers subsequently passed this message on to NIH leadership, as well as to all researchers, health professionals, and others who understand what biomedical research and related sciences can accomplish.

Indeed, Rogers has delivered with increased urgency and directness the R!A message to the nation.

> To keep the hope of research alive, we must inform the public and their elected representatives in understandable and economically defensible terms what the record is of the advances, gains, and benefits obtained from our national investment in research!

Chapter 8

Universal Healthcare: Keeping the Dream Alive

For close to 20 years, Dr. Henry Simmons has been dedicated to the care and feeding of the National Coalition for Health Care (NCHC), a bipartisan, not-for-profit coalition of nonprofit and for-profit healthcare entities seeking better, more affordable healthcare for every American. The inclusive organization was founded in 1986, morphing into its present form in 1990. Its co-chairs, from the start, have been Robert Ray, former Republican governor of Iowa and chief executive officer of the Blue Cross and Blue Shield of Iowa, and the omnipresent Paul Rogers. Former Presidents Ford, Carter, and Bush are honorary co-chairs.

The first Federal health insurance program started early in the history of the nation with the Act for Relief of Sick and Disabled Seamen, 1798. Under this legislation, the government assured all merchant seamen and regular Navy personnel lifetime care at clinics and hospitals located at all major U.S. port cities and controlled locally.

In the 1920s, Sen. Joseph Ransdell (D-La.) tried to muscle up the government's healthcare activities by using the Public Health Service as the vehicle to do so. Many people agree that this marked the opening of the debate on the role of the government in providing health care.

Republican distrust of the government's role in the health arena and general caution of bigger government was evident even then. A Ransdell proposal to create a national institute of health in 1926 stalled for four years. A Republican measure co-sponsored by Ransdell to expand the authority and services of the PHS was passed, but vetoed by President Calvin Coolidge in 1928. In 1930, both bills passed and the rationale for the Federal government's direct involvement in healthcare was established.

Today, more than ever, as the financial noose tightens around the big employers and the middle and lower economic sectors of society in terms of offering or receiving affordable healthcare, strange bedfellows are finding each other. And even as one half-step after another falters or fails, the NCHC keeps the vision alive, refusing to be discouraged by the failure to achieve the necessary policy breakthrough.

Over the years, the organization has held regular meetings of representatives from a broad array of members, and has commissioned expert analytic papers on access to cost and quality of healthcare. It has also attained consensus from its diverse constituency on a series of general principles describing the current condition of the nation's healthcare delivery system and what it would take to improve it. All these activities have been connected to major efforts to conduct grant-supported relevant data collections and policy studies so that the data and collective thinking of NCHC members could be brought to the attention of the public and the body politic.

Critics often question whether any accomplishments have come from these activities. But those involved in NCHC events say that the ongoing education has been more than worthwhile, generating a growing sophistication about health-system problems and challenges among representatives of large corporations, unions, and big insurance payers, in addition to the political analysts, economists, quality-of-care experts, hospital directors, doctors, and nurses who attend or learn about the proceedings.

Obviously, NCHC will never be associated with a successful outcome until America builds a universal coverage system. However, it is safe to say that the steadfast support of Ray and Rogers has kept NCHC alive and its message on the public radar screen. These two private-public figures along with Dr. Simmons and his staff have at times been the sole keepers of the flame.

In 2004, NCHC, now with 95 members representing 130 million constituents, became more specific about the principles and strategies required to

PARKING, ROGERS-STYLE

Downtown Washington, D.C., is not an easy place to get around, and it's even harder to park there. Comments a friend, "You haven't lived until you ride with Paul Rogers to a downtown hotel in Washington, watch him get out of the car with the engine running, and explain to the doorman that the car only needs to be there 30 or 40 minutes. 'Will you be on duty then?,' he asks." This split-second negotiation results in the car being parked on a hotel sidewalk ready for a quick departure by the adroit Mr. Rogers.

move the nation toward basic, universal healthcare coverage. A steady stream of important papers on healthcare cost, quality, and access is now reaching wider audiences through aggressive media outreach. A concerted membership effort is bringing in an impressive group of members, meaning there is much talking back and forth across institutional borders, something new for NCHC members. In 2003, after one of the country's corporate behemoths completed negotiations with its unionized employees, a highly placed corporate executive revealed that his company had joined NCHC at the request of the national union's leader. He pointed out that, in this way, the company would better understand the healthcare issues confronting the workers.

Simmons had occupied high positions in the Department of Health and Human Services during the Nixon Administration. It was here that he met and worked with Congressman Rogers. That is why Rogers was among the first ones Simmons invited into the new organization. According to Simmons, when he laid out his version of a member-driven organization aiming to extend high-quality, basic healthcare to all Americans at a reasonable price, Rogers joined immediately. He made himself consistently available to NCHC as a strategist, recruiter, and public communicator.

Henry Simmons reflects on the contributions of Paul Rogers to this long-term effort. He has come to appreciate Rogers' genuine commitment to healthcare, his apparent total lack of personal ego, and the extraordinary value of his many friends and collaborators from other health-related efforts. Furthermore, Rogers' loyalty seems infinite to him. "Once you're his friend, you are always his friend," explains Simmons.

The lesson here is that Paul Rogers is patient, and, when the stars align, willing to work hard to establish yet another organization to lay the foundation for success in the body politic. He keeps working for what he believes will contribute to a healthier America even when most others get discouraged and despair of ultimate success.

Chapter 9

Long-Term Initiatives

Both as a congressman and as a private citizen, Paul Rogers has a habit of spending some of his time and energy addressing issues and problems whose resolution and solution are likely to come well into the future. Without rehashing what most reasonably informed citizens already know post-9/11, here are two of his most significant current national concerns.

1. The need for major new investments in our local, state, and national public health infrastructure: more highly trained personnel, better information technology and communications capacity, and more research into public health problems.
2. The need for a heightened public education effort to raise awareness and understanding of global health issues and the impact on health of complex environmental changes. To achieve this, we need, at the least, a better understanding of these issues by health professionals—physicians, in particular—and a major new public effort to bring the expert knowledge of specialists in international health and the environmental sciences, other related professionals, and societal opinion-makers and political leaders to bear on the issues.

In the eyes of experts, some of the issues have emerged clearly: for example, the threats from epidemics brought on by increased global interconnectedness (SARS) or by malevolent intent (anthrax). Other concerns, such as the health threat from global warming, have not become front-burner issues for enough leaders or the lay public to produce effective change. Still other aspects of problems and potential challenges suffer from inadequate data to meet one of Rogers' critical benchmarks for selecting action strategies, that is, evidence-based decisions.

The more ambiguous nature of the extent and depth of public health infrastructure deficits allows politicians to talk the talk but fail to make the necessary investments to walk the walk! Furthermore, the potential but immeasurable impact of bioterrorism attacks on health requires speculation, best guesses, and worst-case scenarios of environmental crises (e.g., nuclear war, poisoned water supplies) and global health problems (e.g., malaria).

In addition to these pressures to think beyond our borders, there is the growing bipartisan sense of a dramatic decline internationally in the trust in us as a moral leader. President George W. Bush may well begin addressing some of these concerns in his second term. However, many looking down the road realize that any significant strategy to enhance the world's view of the United States must inevitably include health and education programs. Numerous meetings here and abroad have focused on the kinds of programs that seem to work in developing countries, including U.S. initiatives, and may be prototypes of those to come if we decide to enlarge our national efforts in this area.

First among these prototypes may be the partnership programs instituted by Secretary of State James Baker just after the dramatic collapse of the Soviet Union and his realization that because its only office was in Moscow, the U.S. Agency for International Development (USAID) could not help the Newly Independent States (NIS). Thus he encouraged the creation of a not-for-profit nongovernmental organization, the American International Health Alliance. This nongovernmental organization led by Jim Smith, its president, was able to accept USAID dollars to build partnerships between each of the NIS states with counterpart organizations here. The partnerships have flourished and, instead of disappearing over time, are growing even as they set examples for other organizations to follow. In most instances, even partnerships no longer funded by USAID are continuing because of the enthusiasm and friendship on both sides. Project Hope, led by its new president Dr. John Howe and working largely with privately-raised funds, has added government awards to its portfolio of supporters. Both entities are working in Europe, Asia, and Africa. Project Hope also has activities in Central and South America.

For many years, the China Medical Board has been bringing Western medical education to the Far East. In the past decade, with the leadership of Dr. Roy Schwartz, the board has extended both its substantive and geographical range.

In all of these programs, nurses, dentists, and healthcare administrators share the spotlight with physicians; they are equally important. Undoubtedly, America has vast human, experiential, and material resources to share if those resources are tapped in a coordinated and rational manner. Here is probably where foreign policy comes into direct contact with the healthcare and scientific elements of our society.

HEALTH AS FOREIGN POLICY

To help promote a healthy global environment, Paul Rogers has joined the Board of Directors of the Global Health Council, the most important American nongovernmental group addressing global health issues. Its president and chief executive officer is Dr. Nils Daulaire, former senior health advisor at USAID.

Then, in mid-October 2004, at a dinner party hosted by Rogers and his wife, Becky, Rogers began a post-dinner colloquy. All in attendance thought it would be an eloquent and gracious "goodnight." Instead, Rogers made a passionate and evocative short speech on the need for America to rebuild trust, confidence, and relationships abroad and about the centrality of health and biomedical science to such an effort. He concluded with a challenge to everyone in the room to argue for including health in our foreign policy.

The brief discussion afterward made it evident that everyone saw the wisdom of working together through their various professional affiliations on the broad issues raised by Rogers. The group has met again and continues to expand the circle of politically relevant influential people who already learned of the wide range of existing efforts among those entities thrust together by Rogers.

In the old days, tackling these problems, which seem to defy an easy solution, would have probably constituted a long-term investment. Today's fast-paced environment, Rogers points out, requires rapid response even when a solution has long-term implications.

Thus, in the cause of bioterrorism protection, Rogers has brought leaders in the public health professions together with Research!America and the Association of Academic Health Centers, seeking to break down any walls between them and establishing de facto teams for activation and further work as needed.

To further his health goals, Paul Rogers has been chair and now co-chair of an Institute of Medicine Roundtable on Environmental Health since its inception five years ago. The roundtable brings together scientists, practitioners, other health professionals, and members of the public to raise the level of education on environmental health issues across the board. Rogers' mantra is that to convince America to improve its investment in and behavior concerning environmental protection, everyone in this endeavor must think of environmental issues primarily in terms of human health.

When Rogers became convinced that our environmental policies were misdirected, he followed through on his conviction that data and expertise must inform the best policy reformulation. He agreed to chair the Roundtable (formerly, the Forum) on Health and the Environment at the National Academy of Sciences. Over the past five years, the organization has brought expert knowledge and data to public attention on a wide variety of environmental issues. It has also been a public venue to explore various, sometimes competing, strategies for solutions. Finally, it has been a place where Paul Rogers can implement his message: "There will be no progress in national environmental policies and behavior without a convincing linkage of the impact upon human health that the policy change would produce."

THE CENTERS FOR DISEASE CONTROL AND PREVENTION

With the doubling of NIH's budget accomplished, Rogers turned to improving funding for public health. On September 29, 2004, at a meeting of invited guests knowledgeable about science and health, Paul Rogers and Evan Jones, chief executive officer of DiGene Corporation and the president of the Campaign for Public Health, introduced the purposes and goals of their new organization, laying the groundwork for inviting those present to join in the effort.

ANOTHER MEAL, ANOTHER FRIEND

One day, Rogers and a friend were out looking for a nice place to have lunch. They came upon a restaurant with an inviting name but a long entry line. Rogers slipped by the crowd and went inside. He greeted the restaurant hostess warmly, and he introduced himself: "I'm Congressman Paul Rogers, and my very special friend here has come to join me at the table that we have reserved." They were seated in a flash.

The lunch was delicious, and the service was flawless. When the two were well out the front door, Rogers abruptly hurried back into the restaurant. He had forgotten to say goodbye to the hostess. Thanking her generously, he said he would be back again soon.

When his friend asked him how long he had been coming to the restaurant, Rogers said he had never been there and that he and the hostess had never seen each other before. "But she knows me now!" he added, and commented that he made many new friends in Washington this way.

The campaign's raison d'être is to advocate with a unified voice for an increase in the budget of the Centers for Disease Control and Prevention (CDC) from $7 million to $15 billion by the year 2010.

Rogers personally recruited all 10 advisors to the campaign from among the R!A's most influential members cognizant of the issues facing the nation post-9/11.

CDC, an institution synonymous with public health around the world, was established in 1946 in Atlanta, Georgia, as the Communicable Disease Center, a branch of the Public Health Service. Before long, the agency enlarged its original scope from controlling malaria in southeastern military training areas to controlling communicable diseases in the United States and its territories.

In the years since, CDC fought to control numerous diseases, among them typhus, polio, smallpox, AIDS, Legionnaire's disease, and Ebola virus. When the agency broadened its mission from stemming disease to preventing disease, it took on the problems of chronic disease, behavioral illness (e.g., child abuse, alcoholism), and environmental hazards. When the agency accepted responsibility for protecting Earth from moon germs and vice-versa, CDC's mission stretched into space.* Most recently, the agency has been collaborating with pharmaceutical companies to stockpile drugs, vaccines, and other supplies needed in the event of bioterrorism attacks.

The agency's name, but not its acronym, has changed a few times over the years. In 1970, CDC had come to stand for the Center for Disease Control; in 1981, Center became "Centers" to encompass its field centers across the country, each with special expertise; in 1992, the words "and Prevention" were added. By law, the acronym may not be changed.

THE NATIONAL LIBRARY OF MEDICINE

Paul Rogers has also been involved for many years in the development and support of the National Library of Medicine. A long-time friend of its director, Dr. Donald Lindberg, and chair of the Friends of the NLM, Rogers has a good grasp of the library's crucial role in helping elevate the health and science potential of the information technology revolution.

The National Library of Medicine is currently poised to assume a critical role in the dissemination of biomedical information to researchers, health professionals, and the general public both here and abroad. This invaluable resource has come a long way since its humble beginnings in 1836: A single bookcase in the Office of the Surgeon General of the Army in Washington, D.C.

Eight years later, its first catalogue listed 2,100 books. But in 1865, Lieutenant John Shaw Billings, a surgeon and book lover, took over the library. When he retired 30 years later, he had transformed it into the world's

* CDC makes certain that every item worn or carried into space is sterilized. When the spacecraft returns, everything and everyone abroad go into isolation until CDC certifies they are germ-free.

greatest collection of medical literature from every era and nation. The first comprehensive index of medical journal articles, *Index Medicus*, started by Lieutenant Billings, was the precursor to NLM's online database, MEDLINE. Originally intended to serve as a resource for military physicians, the library, under Billings, was gradually opened to health professionals everywhere.

In the decades since, Congress expanded NLM's work to include administering grants to medical libraries around the country, developing a host of computerized research services for health professionals, and providing consumer-friendly online listings of clinical trials. The clinical-trial listing is part of NLM's increasing role in educating and informing the public.

The library, located on the campus of the National Institutes of Health, is also now working with the U.S. Centers for Disease Control and Prevention to use information technology to bring more biomedical resources to the American people.

Recognizing the deep interest of former House Speaker Newt Gingrich (R-Ga.) in information technology, the NLM Board of Regents asked Rogers to speak to Gingrich in mid-October 2004 and urge him to join the board, and also to co-chair the group's Strategic Planning Committee. Gingrich recalled how all this had come to pass. Discovering one day that his schedule included a telephone call from Paul Rogers, he spent much of the time beforehand trying to anticipate what Rogers might ask for. Whatever it was, he knew that he would probably say "Yes"! He was never able to say "No" to Paul Rogers.

And, indeed, once Rogers connected the dots between Gingrich's interest and growing expertise in IT with the reality and potential of the NLM, Gingrich enthusiastically agreed to come on board.

As the second Bush term evolves, the odds are that the one health issue that will have bipartisan support is the move toward the electronic medical record and associated public and professional IT derivatives. Thus, Gingrich's new role could prove brilliantly effective.

The electronic medical record, a computer-based patient history of care—which can include billing and claim records, digitized patient imaging records, and other relevant medical information—may be a major factor in making healthcare available to all of America. First used by the military, it made telemedicine conferencing possible, allowed for remote monitoring of a patient's biological functions, and enabled moving a soldier's medical records along with the soldier. A 10-year plan to develop a health-information infrastructure was announced by the Department of Health and Human Services in July 2004. It may result in cost savings of such significance as to make universal healthcare possible. Up-front costs would be steep, but HHS Secretary Tommy Thompson estimated that a nationwide system could lower the country's annual healthcare costs by 10 percent.

PART III

The Essence of Leadership

Rogers in full sartorial splendor, his feet planted firmly in his home state. Once just another congressman from Florida, Rogers became the nation's health-law guru. This combination sketch and collage was a gift to Becky and Paul Rogers from the artist Lang Auerbach in 1978, the year before Paul retired from Congress.

Chapter 10

The Making of a True Leader

The sum of what Paul Rogers has created is even greater than all its parts. Only on taking a step back and observing the entire panorama, can one see a significant change in the landscape. Reflecting on what Rogers has achieved over so many years of concentrated effort, one is invariably impressed with the nature of his leadership skills. Jeff Schwartz remembers:

> I don't think it was all intellectual on Rogers' part. Some of it was instinctive and characterological. It was the kind of person he is. That is why everybody warmed to him so much. It wasn't a tactic on his part. It was Paul being Paul, it was genuine and people got that about him.

And it was one of the qualities that helped to make Paul Rogers the superior leader he is today.

It seems important, therefore, to compare Rogers with some of the more important leadership models advocated by scholars and exemplified by major leadership figures.

Over the centuries, a wide variety of experts have explored the qualities, behavior, and standards of leaders. Here we look at the work of a selected, but representative, sample of writing on modern organizational leadership by scholars who have examined this phenomenon through the lens of history, psychology, and corporate success. We then consider the insights that some physician-philosophers on humankind can offer to future leaders: the search for meaning, the nature of human interaction, expanding one's horizons, and husbanding our energies wisely. Last, we provide a near-perfect example of a leader, Florence Nightingale, nurse-extraordinaire, whose selfless efforts on behalf of suffering humanity led her from nursing to work in public health and administration and eventually into political action and advocacy.

One way to begin a discussion of leadership is to indicate what an exemplary leader is not. Historian, political scientist, and leadership guru James MacGregor Burns does this in his book, *Leadership*, where he tells the interesting story of Niccolo Machiavelli (1469–1527).[1] After a leadership career in the young republican government of Florence, Machiavelli wrote an infamous book on how to wield political power, *The Prince*. Published after the author's death and privately circulated, *The Prince* garnered such fame and notoriety that within a relatively few years it was condemned by the Roman Catholic Church and placed on the church's index of forbidden books.

Among Machiavelli's precepts for gaining and keeping political power were, first, that the prince, as a leader, must always appear merciful, faithful, totally honest, humane, and religious. Second, the leader must be ruthless and deceitful in achieving his goals. Third, enemies should receive the most punishment possible; a dead enemy cannot do the prince any harm. Fourth, the prince must learn to eliminate any emotional connection on his part to individual competitors or enemies and seek only to manipulate them as things rather than people.

Burns believes it plausible, if not likely, that Machiavelli's privately circulated tract was actually a veiled criticism of the Medici prince who retook power in Florence from the republic of Florence in 1512, using a Spanish army. Machiavelli had risen rapidly in the republican government of Florence and, as defense minister, had replaced its mercenary army with a citizens' militia. Many people at the time, according to Burns, doubted that Machiavelli meant what he said in *The Prince*. After being tortured on the rack, stripped bare, and exiled from the city,

Machiavelli was in no mood to give the prince any excuse to throw him back on the rack. So, although in his book Machiavelli seems to be teaching the prince how to behave, he might actually have been describing how the prince did behave.

The damage wrought by amoral and scandalous exercises of raw power and deceit—from the accounting scandals of the late 1990s to the Iraq war—has prompted some writers to pick up on the relevance of Machiavelli to some of today's business, institution, and government leaders. Robert Wright is a scholar, senior fellow at the New American Foundation, and author of *Nonzero: The Logic of Human Destiny.* In an op-ed article the summer before the 2004 Presidential election, he refers to Machiavelli when he proposes a way that Presidential contender John Kerry might overcome the charge that he was a "waffler."[2]

> Maybe what he [Kerry] needs to do is to take on a sensitive, complicated problem, lay down a core conviction, and stick with it through thick and thin.
>
> By the way, Machiavelli might approve. Though he favored fear over love, he said that being feared and loved is the best situation of all. And failing that, "a leader at least ought to inspire fear in such a way that, if he does not win love, he avoids hatred." (p. A21)

In *American Dynasty*, economic and political commentator and former Republican political strategist Kevin Phillips writes extensively about Machiavelli's influence on both Lee Atwater and Karl Rove, the former a key political advisor to the first President Bush, the latter an advisor to both President George H. W. Bush and President George W. Bush.[3]

Lest the reader think that these observations pertain only to Republicans, one need only recall similar tactics used by the other side in the 2004 Presidential election campaign. One oft-heard conclusion among the American electorate is that the "other side" or "both sides" behaved in a Machiavellian manner. Whether Machiavelli wrote *The Prince* in jest or in all seriousness, it is in the latter vein that Burns criticizes him vigorously: "More than mere selfishness, at the core of Machiavellianism lay the most pernicious and inhuman concept of all: the treatment of other persons, other leaders, as things." (p. 446)

In other words, Machiavelli's tract called for manipulating people rather than working with them. Further, he implies that empathizing with others can lead one to identify with their view rather than to impose one's own view. But, says Burns, "It is precisely that—identifying with the point of view of followers—that makes the transforming leader, in the long run, far more effective than manipulators." (p. 446)

Burns describes teaching others how to manipulate people as merely "transactional." If you take *The Prince* at face value, suggests Burns, it can be viewed as the first in a long line of how-to books for would-be leaders, like Dale Carnegie's *How to Win Friends and Influence People.* Instead of teaching transformational leadership, which depends on collaboration, they espouse transactional leadership, which is rooted in authoritarianism.

Furthermore, Burns believes that transformational leadership can be taught and that such leadership and education can coalesce at the point where more and more leaders are being educated and then replicating the process with others.

> Fully-sharing leaders perceive their roles as shaping the future to the advantage of groups with which they identify, an advantage they identify in terms of the broadest possible goals and the highest possible levels of morality. (p. 448)

Burns goes on to argue that without a symbiosis between strong leadership and an active citizenry, we may well face a crisis in the quality of both leadership and citizenship. "Leadership is collective. One-man leadership is a contradiction in terms." (p. 452)

Leadership is also causative and transformational; leadership is "event-making," says Burns. It stimulates the creation of a new entity that may continue to exert moral leadership after the original creative leaders are gone. (He seems clearly to have the Founding Fathers in mind!) Finally, true leadership, for Burns, is not only morally purposeful and goal-oriented, but also elevating for both leaders and followers.

A decade ago, psychologist Daniel Goleman posited the neurosciences concept of an open limbic system within the brain that allows humans to take in external stimuli and incorporate these messages into their own decision-making process.[4] More recently, he joined with colleagues Richard

Boyatzis and Annie McKee to describe an attribute of leadership that builds on this concept. In *Primal Leadership*, they explore the process by which a decision is made to follow a particular person's lead.[5] Some examples of the stimuli that Goleman and his co-authors feel can attract followers are Ronald Reagan's affability, Bill Cosby's benign insouciance, and Mother Teresa's goodness and other-directedness. The authors assign the label "primal leader" to those people endowed with the capacity to enter effectively into the limbic systems of other people. This ability, in turn, leads to resonance between leader and follower.

A FUTILE EFFORT

During a week-long automobile tour of France, Paul Rogers' legendary ability to reach across any and all barriers to communication was sorely tested. Becky and the congressman were traveling with friends Jackie and David Challoner. Although Jackie was the only one in the group who could speak French, it was Paul who always rushed out of the car to pay for the gas and, if possible, to chat awhile.

One day in a remote village in the French Alps, this scenario repeated itself, but this time the gas station attendant's response was, "Je ne parle pas l'anglais. Je ne sais pas. . . . Non comprender." Undeterred, Paul kept up his end of the conversation, possibly trying to bridge the chasm between the two countries and maybe even get this guy to come to Palm Beach someday and spend a few Euros. The more bewildered the attendant became, the more intense Paul became as he tried to make himself understood.

When the attendant rolled his eyes toward the auto as if to ask, "Does this guy belong to you? Is he crazy?" the passengers couldn't stop laughing long enough to help either man. Somehow Rogers managed to pay for his gas and return happily to the car, leaving an even happier attendant behind.

Such an ability, they believe, is not always inborn; it can be learned. An example is when people take on a personally transcendent cause to which they can become committed, and then win others over to the same purpose. The authors identify six styles of leadership and describe how they resonate, as follows:

1. *Visionary*: Moves people toward shared dreams.
2. *Coaching*: Connects individual's goals with an organization's goals.

3. *Affiliative*: Creates harmony by connecting people to each other.
4. *Democratic*: Values people's input and gets commitment through participation.
5. *Pacesetting*: Meets challenging and exciting goals.
6. *Commanding*: Soothes fears by giving clear direction in an emergency.

Resonance, they declare, can be achieved in the first four styles; but it is difficult, if not impossible, to achieve in the remaining two models. Perhaps this is because these qualities, with their authoritarian connotation, can override some of the spirit of transformational leadership.

In the landmark study *Good to Great*, James Collins, a noted teacher and consultant on leadership, looks into why some companies never go beyond just being good.[6] The study was undertaken after a successful corporate leader, profiled by Collins in *Built to Last*, suggested that Collins next study ways on how already excellent corporations can improve their performance.[7]

Collins and his researchers took up the challenge. First, they defined "best" in business-success terms (i.e., the best-performing companies on the Fortune 500 list that consistently outperformed the average annual performance of the Fortune 500 population over a 15-year period). They then analyzed about a dozen corporations that fell into the "good" rather than the "best" category. Many of the findings were unexpected. For example, although well-known in the business world, the companies that rated highest were not among the most prominent and visible. Neither were their leaders among the nation's best-known business leaders; certainly, none were household names like Jack Welch, Lee Iacocca, and Donald Trump.

Despite the team's assumption that leadership style did not account for much, they found that when it came to achieving and sustaining "best" status, company leadership style did matter. Furthermore, the leaders of the best-performing companies had much in common. According to Collins, there is a five-level hierarchy among leaders. All the best leaders functioned at Level 5, a commonality expressed by the Collins team in the formula, professional will + humility = Level 5 leadership. The Collins Hierarchy is as follows:[8]

Level 1 *(highly capable individual)* Makes productive contributions through talent, knowledge, skills, and good work habits.

Level 2 *(contributing team member)* Contributes individual capabilities to the achievement of group objectives and works effectively with others in a group setting.

Level 3 *(competent manager)* Organizes people and resources toward the effective and efficient pursuit of predetermined objectives.

Level 4 *(effective leader)* Catalyzes commitment to and vigorous pursuit of a clear and compelling vision, stimulating higher performance standards.

Level 5 *(executive)* Builds enduring greatness through a paradoxical blend of personal humility and professional will.

In general, the leadership characteristics that made for Level 5 status were a quiet, but persistent drive toward meeting the company goals and a sharing-the-credit attitude, eschewing the lion's share of the credit for meeting corporate goals. Thus, the Level 5 leader is constantly sprinkling credit across the rest of the leadership cadre and to the employees in general.*

The team's finding was empirical, not ideological. "We were not looking for Level 5 leadership in our research, or anything like it," report the investigators, "but the data was overwhelming and convincing." (p. 10)

They identified one of the "most damaging trends in recent history" as "the tendency (especially by boards of directors) to select dazzling, celebrity leaders and to de-select potential Level 5 leaders." (p. 39)

Every good-to-great company in their study "had Level 5 leadership during the pivotal transition years. . . . Larger-than-life, celebrity leaders

* Michael Maccoby, a psychoanalyst and anthropologist, has much practical experience with the world's best-known corporate leaders. In a conversation with me (Bulger), he pointed out that the corporations Collins studied were not among the biggest and most complex. To lead global corporations of great scale, Maccoby holds, probably requires the grand egos of narcissistic CEOs. I (Bulger) suspect people who run for President of the United States probably fall into that category, as would Napoleon, Alexander the Great, Winston Churchill, and Charles de Gaulle. We apparently need our great narcissistic and sometimes messianic leaders, but we need transformational leadership even more.

who ride in from the outside are negatively correlated with going from good to great." (p. 10)

Indeed, "10 of 11 good-to-great CEOs came from inside the company, whereas the comparison companies tried outside CEOs six times more often." Collins writes, "I believe that potential Level 5 leaders exist all around us, if we just know what to look for, and that many people have the potential to evolve into Level 5." (p. 39)

THE PSYCHOLOGICAL UNDERPINNINGS OF A LEADER'S CHARACTER

Viktor Frankl, a psychiatrist trained by Freud, wrote the short masterpiece, *Man's Search for Meaning,* while incarcerated in Auschwitz during World War II.[9] From that experience, he learned that although his jailers could strip him of food, clothes, dignity, family, profession, and even a reason for hope in the future, they could not compromise or minimize the untouchable human core—the intrinsic quest for meaning.

Thus, Frankl came to posit the search for personal meaning as the central force in the development of the individual psyche. Relating this concept to leadership development, one can see its connection to leadership behavior, that is, leaders fulfilling their own personal quest for meaning by reaching out with ideas and goals that touch a similar quest in others.*

In *Making Contact,* clinical psychiatrist Leston Havens describes human intersections, reproducing verbatim conversations with patients.[10] During these interactions he sets forth his goal in psychotherapy, namely, to demonstrate that two people can occupy "the same space," coexisting without feeling the need to either invade or want to be invaded by the other. Havens has focused his attention on the essence of a healthy interpersonal relationship and sees it not just as therapeutic, but also as a way of thinking about relations between ethnic, racial, and other groups, including those involved in international relations.

---

* In this vein, it is interesting to note that in early 2004, geneticist Dean Hamer of the National Cancer Institute reported identifying a gene that inclines human beings to embrace a belief in some higher power.[11]

In Havens' construct, leaders would not try to dominate or force others to join them. Rather, they would seek to enter into a collaborative relationship where shared goals are pursued for mutual benefit. Thus, in a competitive environment, a Havens-like leader would not seek to invade or destroy a competitor, but rather wish the competitor the best for the future. Along with Goleman and Collins, Havens argues that the interactive tools of leadership can be learned. Havens, therefore, might encourage us to develop a leadership measure that assesses the nature of personal interactions between the leader and followers.

George L. Engel, another clinician, enlarged the canvas on which the picture of healthcare and health status is to be painted by connecting the dots between molecular events and the psychological and social influences upon illness—and in so doing made famous his construct of the biopsychosocial model.[12] One can assume that, from Engel's perspective, health leaders should demonstrate an understanding of all influences on the health status of individuals and populations, not just those that flow from their own narrow area of professional expertise.

In recent years, Senator Bill Frist (R-Tenn.) has broadened his professional reach beyond his background as a heart surgeon to include consideration of all the biopsychosocial and environmental factors and policies that affect health. He is an example of how someone can quickly rise in national influence by showing expertise in the determinants of health along with a public health-centered view of policy issues. In his first term as senator, he rose to the post of Senate majority leader, the first person in history to do so this quickly and the first physician to serve in this post.

When it comes to helping those in leadership positions cope with adversity and sustain a pervasive optimism, one aphorism from the many writings of Sir William Osler (1849–1919) keeps coming to mind: "Live your life in day-tight compartments," he advised students and colleagues.[13] Considered by many to be one of the greatest doctors who ever lived, in part because of his humanism, Osler held that each day should absorb all our energy with no thought of tomorrow. Replaying yesterday's failures while worrying about tomorrow's problems makes the burden of living today almost insurmountable. Living each day to its fullest provides a focus on the tasks at hand and an implicit awareness that each day brings something new. Soon, the days add up to weeks, and the weeks add up to years, leading to a happy, productive life.

Osler, whose influence was felt far beyond England, Canada, and the United States where he practiced and taught medicine, also espoused developing imperturbability—a steadiness of hand and a coolness of nerve, a calmness amid storm—when treating patients. A physician who does otherwise, he warns, soon loses his patient's confidence. Lest this harden into callousness, Osler went on to caution against "hardening the human heart by which we live."[14]

Osler also set the standard for evidence-based practice in the first comprehensive medical textbook based on science and observation in the English-speaking world. Largely derived from his clinical experience as an internist and on the more than 1,000 autopsies that he carried out, *Principles and Practice of Medicine** set a pattern for reviewing each disease historically, including the requisite details of diagnosis, course of the disease if untreated, and current recommended treatments—laced with his skeptical views of many accepted treatments.

While acknowledging the role of environmental and other factors in the spread of disease, Osler was a passionate preventionist who rallied adherents to his cause. Speaking before an audience of primarily medical students in Edinburgh shortly after the British Parliament's repeal of compulsory smallpox vaccination, he offered to take three members of the British Parliament, three anti-vaccination doctors (if any could be found), and four anti-vaccinationists to help him in the next smallpox epidemic.[15] He then promised to care for those who later contracted the illness and also ensured ceremonious funerals for the three or four of them likely to die.†

* This book, first published in 1892, was reprinted around the world, coming out periodically as either a single- or multi-authored text until the 1940s.

† In this address, Osler also introduced his concept of three gospels: one concerning our relationship with spirit, one covering our relationship to the material world, and the third about our relationship to our bodies. It is in his overview of the extraordinary 19th-century social advances that he argues that man has redeemed man.

At the start of World War I, a few years later, Osler took his case to the troops—literally. He addressed a contingent of British soldiers on the efficiency and safety of typhoid vaccination, thus causing a major debate in Parliament.*

Florence Nightingale (1820–1910) is another exemplar of transformational leadership.[16] One of two sisters born into a privileged, well-to-do English family, Florence, in contrast to her sister, did not like the life of the countrified gentlewoman, instead turning to her books and her studies. A personal seminal event at age 17, which she felt was a religious calling to reduce human suffering, eventually led her to nursing. In her early 30s, she founded a nursing school in Germany that offered what she deemed an adequate education. Her consequent career as a nurse rapidly led to her being asked to go to the front in the Crimean War, where she completely revamped practices of battlefield care.

Eschewing public attention (like any good Level 5 leader), she slipped back into England quietly.

Settling by herself in a centrally located London apartment, she refused an invitation from Queen Victoria to live and work in Buckingham Palace. Her argument was that she needed to be more easily accessible to visits from government officials, ambassadors, and health officials from around the world than would be the case if she were sequestered at Buckingham Palace. She spent most of the rest of her life writing extensively, building administrative and public health plans, and pursuing political advocacy to reduce widespread disease and suffering throughout the world.

There is no doubt that Nightingale's leadership message is to place the public's interest above professional bias to improve the lot of others.

Her *Notes on Nursing*, for example, first published in 1860, was aimed at the more than 25,000 English homebodies who categorized themselves as nurses, instructing them on how to give proper care in the home. Within a month, 15,000 copies were sold and, shortly thereafter, Nightingale's dream was fulfilled with the formal establishment of a school of nursing in London.

---

* Compulsory typhoid vaccination for servicemen was never made official policy in Great Britain. Compulsory smallpox vaccination was restored.

Nightingale started schools of nursing and midwifery, which spread to 13 countries in Europe, Asia, and the Americas. She redesigned and reshaped hospital organization to cut down on the transmission of disease, helped prevent millions of premature deaths in India by designing sanitation systems, and created new institutions and new arrangements to achieve the health and public health goals she was pursuing. She also built on her arithmetic skills to connect improved health status to prevention and health-promotion advances based upon solid epidemiology—all this in recognition of her underlying purpose to reduce human suffering through whatever venues she could. Thus, as a health leader, she successfully transcended her initial professional base in pursuing her ultimate goal.

Another example of a health leader who has stayed true to his goals is Dr. C. Everett Koop. As surgeon general of the United States from 1982 to 1989, he followed science to develop public-policy conclusions and went on to fight for them even if they were sometimes different from his personal philosophy and the political positions of his own party.

There are also otherwise-transformational leaders who have sometimes reverted to a purely transactional mode, much to society's detriment. According to some accounts, in 1994 President Clinton felt that his worst political mistake up to that point was failing to join with Senator Bob Dole (R-Kans.) in a bipartisan approach to providing health coverage for everyone, a Federal program they both wanted. Placing presidential ambitions or parochial politics, or both, above the goal of making healthcare equitable and accessible to all is a failure in Level 5 leadership.

One may reasonably ask what single major lesson comes from all these models and examples of leadership successes and leadership failures. For me (Bulger) two brief thoughts are right on the mark.

Writes Burns, "In real life the most practical advice for leaders is not to treat pawns like pawns, princes like princes, but all persons like persons."

Woodrow Wilson called for leaders who, by boldly interpreting a nation's conscience, could lift a people out of their everyday selves. That people can be lifted into their better selves is the secret of transforming leadership. These thoughts from Burns and Wilson delineate the setting where Lestor Havens meets Viktor Frankl in the person of Paul Rogers.

Chapter 11

The Rogers Model

It was on the morning of June 12, 2001. Beneath a white tent in front of Building 1, the first building erected on its now 310-acre campus, the National Institutes of Health in Bethesda, Maryland, dedicated the institute's main plaza to Paul Rogers. The ceremony honoring Mr. Health took place close to the spot where Franklin D. Roosevelt, a year before the United States was drawn into World War II, dedicated the NIH grounds to "life conservation, rather than life destruction."*

No one seems to know what has made Rogers such a noble advocate for the best possible health for all Americans (although the word *dedication* easily springs to mind). Most people agree, however, that he is thoughtful, considerate, and respectful of others' opinions. He is an excellent orator; he

---

* Among his other remarks, he declared, "We cannot be a strong nation unless we are a healthy nation. And so we must recruit not only men and materials, but also knowledge and science in the service of national strength." Roosevelt outlined plans for government grants to researchers working in private universities and labs, addressing the public's concern about governmental controls in the medical arena by saying that there were no plans to "socialize medical practice any more than there was a plan to socialize industry." In his closing remarks, he put forth this vision: "I voice for America, and for the stricken world, our hopes, our prayers, our faith in the power of man's humanity to man."

is persuasive in argument and decisive when the time comes; and he seems to have a special skill for determining when that time has come.

In the political arena, Paul Rogers insists on hard evidence, clear analysis, and arguments from all sides before taking a position. He works hard at building a winning coalition before pressing for a conclusion. He does not like to lose, but neither does he take pleasure in anyone else's losing. Thus, it is logical to conclude that he is happiest when he wins and his opponents come away feeling they have been fairly and respectfully treated, and that they might even get his support when the next issue comes around. At the dedication ceremony, Steve Lawton shared memories of his boss.

> Once you've worked for Paul Rogers, you always work for Paul Rogers. He called me last week. He said, "Lawton, how about getting up a few remarks for me for this NIH dedication?" I said, "Boss, this time I've got my own speech to write, and you're not getting a word of it."
>
> A Rogers awards ceremony is hardly a unique event. Paul Rogers has received many prestigious awards, including the Lasker Award, the Public Welfare Medal of the National Academy of Sciences, and fifteen honorary academic degrees.* But I strongly suspect that for him, this is the granddaddy of them all: The Paul G. Rogers Plaza, gracing the lawn of the world's premier biomedical research institution, which he helped build, guide, and protect, both while in Congress and as a private citizen—serving on the board of the American Cancer Society and the Friends of the National Library of Medicine, and as chairman of a revitalized Research!America, leading the fight on behalf of the biomedical research community for a doubling of the NIH budget while Congressman John Porter successfully led the fight on Capitol Hill.
>
> It is so appropriate that Paul Rogers now joins other Congressional giants recognized on these grounds—Magnuson, Hatfield, Natcher, Stokes, and Porter, among others, for whom buildings have been named. But this is significant: He is the first legislative committee chairman to be so honored. (The other members of Congress were honored as chairs of their Health Appropriations Subcommittee.)

---

* A list of honorary degrees, awards, and organizational affiliations appears in Appendix B.

All of you know of the incredible legislative achievements accomplished by the subcommittee chaired by Paul Rogers during only eight years. During his chairmanship, there were threats to the fabric of the National Institutes of Health, some well-meaning and some not so well-meaning. During his initial tenure as chair, legislation to separate the National Cancer Institute from the rest of the NIH passed the Senate, 91-1, with the support of the President. Having previously headed a special NIH oversight committee, Rogers was already well known for his knowledge of health and biomedical research issues. He knew that the Senate's approach to the War on Cancer threatened the interdisciplinary nature of research, no matter how laudable the intentions.

Weeks of hearings, including testimony by several Nobel Laureates, demonstrated that research in one disease area has an impact on research in another area. The ultimate National Cancer Act of 1971 created an enhanced National Cancer Institute within the NIH—holding the institutes together, ensuring collaboration among them and among NIH grantees. Speaking before the Rogers subcommittee three years after the act was passed, the proponents of the Senate approach testified that the bill crafted by Paul Rogers and his colleagues was the right strategy for waging the war on cancer.

In the 1970s, the concept of peer review was misunderstood and threatened by the White House. Executive Branch submissions to Congress proposed terminating merit review of grants as well as research training grants. Paul Rogers' answer was to hold well-publicized hearings demonstrating the importance of peer review by independent experts and detailing the critical role of training grants in fostering young research careers. It comes as no surprise that peer review and training grants are now statutory requirements.

Even during contentious hearings, Paul Rogers demonstrated grace, courtliness, and respect for differing positions. The man has style. His command of the gavel was substantial, but the subcommittee debates were always fair, with efforts made to accommodate the other side. Because he welcomed contributions to legislation by other subcommittee members, well over half of the bills reported by the subcommittee were by unanimous vote. A few months ago, I found myself on an elevator with Casper Weinberger. Weinberger was HHS Secretary during the contentious Nixon years, and there had been classic confrontations on Capitol Hill over the proper role of the Federal government in the area of health, and the prerogatives of the Executive and Legislative Branches of government in crafting health policy.

Paul Rogers and Casper Weinberger had gone toe-to-toe during hearings on President Nixon's proposals to terminate many Federal health initiatives. Indeed, the hearings were always heated. Referring to Weinberger's tenure as head of the Office of Management and Budget during Nixon's budget cuts, for example, Rogers said to Weinberger at the first hearing: "I hear you graduated in subtraction."

Weinberger was a formidable witness. When I told him, that I had worked for Paul Rogers, he quickly responded: "He was a great chairman, a great public servant." There was no rancor, only respect for an able adversary.

There is a "Rogers bar" in Washington, made up of those of us who served him. We are in law firms, public health organizations, trade associations, consulting firms. Paul Rogers is the calling card for each of us. Justified or not, the reputation of people who begin their careers working for public figures derives from the character of the people for whom they have worked. And these impressions are based not so much on our mentors' politics as it is on their ethics, their honesty, their fairness to others. Scores of us owe our success to Paul Rogers for the opportunities he gave us and for what he taught us. But most important, we owe him for lending us his reputation.

So I say to Paul Rogers: On behalf of those who were honored to serve you while you served this country, not a day goes by when we don't think of you. Not a week goes by when we don't ask ourselves, "What would Paul Rogers have done?" And not a month goes by when we don't tell someone, with great pride, "I used to work for Paul Rogers."

Your lifetime achievements—crafting legislation protecting the public health, fostering biomedical research, clean air and safe drinking water, and so many other laws—have laid the foundation for incredible advances in the health of this nation and a cleaner environment. The full impact of your work is still unknown. Your contributions will reach far into this new millennium.

Thank you for what you have done for this great institution, and for our country. But thank you also for being a mentor (at times, even a father) to so many of us, showing us how to conduct ourselves, how to serve, and how to live.

In Rogers' years as a legislator, his staff would frequently urge him to build a winning case before they called a hearing, a tactic that might then lead directly to legislation the congressman could author or advocate. Instead, Rogers would often hear first from the leading opponents on the issue, treating them with great kindness and openness and providing them with enough time to make their point. He wanted them as friends on future issues. "It only makes sense," explains Rogers, "that to get a bill through Congress, you have to work both sides."

Elected to Congress as a conservative Democrat, Rogers nevertheless came to see the need for government support when it came to matters of health, the environment, and related biomedical research. Therefore his name is on numerous health and environmental laws that the most liberal Democrat might be proud of. Moreover, many conservatives (both Democrat and Republican) have lent their support and name to his efforts.

STRATEGY NOT TACTICS

Former staffer, Jeff Schwartz, suggests a reason why Rogers was such an effective leader: "Paul had the kind of wisdom that was about winning the war, not winning the battles. Never burn your bridges. Always keep a degree of cordiality and respect, even when you're in fundamental disagreement. In the end, that will serve both your own policy goals and the instituion much better."

To this day, Rogers has a way of finding the argument that transcends political party and philosophy, asking people to give primacy to the impact of a suggested course of action on the American people before bringing other considerations into the picture.

Congressman Dr. Tim Lee Carter (R-Ky.) did just that once at great personal risk to his own political career. A congressman and a ranking minority member of Rogers' committee, he was persuaded to vote in favor of the Emergency Health Personnel Act, a bill extending the scope of the National Health Service Corps by providing for contracts for physician-assistant education and deployment to underserved areas. Rogers had swayed him. Instead of couching his argument in the words of an advocate of government-sponsored medical care, Rogers had taken another tack. The new provisions would not threaten existing practitioners, said Rogers; the fact is that doctors, already carrying a full patient load, could not take care of the large number of poor people with no access to primary care physicians. By adding more clinicians to the National Health Service Corps in medically underserved areas, the proposed legislation would

Table 1
Paul Rogers According to Burns, Goleman, et al, and Collins

AUTHOR	ATTRIBUTE
Burns	Transformational leadership can be taught; new leaders are created or enabled, or both.
	Leadership is not one person: it is a collection of leaders.
	Leadership is contentious; it involves some conflict and creative tension.
	Leadership is causative, it makes things happen.
	Leadership is purposeful and goal-oriented.
	Transforming leadership is felt as personally elevating.
Goleman, Boyatzis, and McKee	Self-awareness: self-assessment, self-confidence.
	Self-management: self-control, transparency, optimism.
	Social awareness: empathy, organizational awareness, service.
	Relationship management: inspiration, influence, developing others, change catalyst, teamwork, and collaboration.
	Uses each of the six leadership styles (visionary, coaching, affiliative, democratic, pacesetting, commanding) in a prudent, appropriate manner.
Collins	Personal humility: ■ Demonstrates a compelling modesty, never boastful. ■ Acts with quiet, calm, determination; relies on inspired standards, not inspiring charisma, to motivate. ■ Channels ambition into the company, not the self; sets up successors for even greater success in the next generation. ■ Looks out the window, not in the mirror to apportion credit for success of company–to others, external factors, and good luck.
	Professional will: ■ Creates superb results. ■ Manifests an unwavering resolve to do what must be done to produce best long-term results. ■ Sets standard for building an enduring institution. ■ Looks in mirror, not out the window, to apportion responsibility for poor results, never blaming others, external factors, or bad luck.

Table 2
Paul Rogers According to Frankl, Engel, Oster, Havens, and Nightingale

AUTHOR	ATTRIBUTE
Frankl, Osler	Finds meaning in following a superordinate goal.
Engel, Nightingale, Osler	Understands the breadth of health determinants from molecular to bio-psychosocial (including environmental) elements.
Nightingale, Osler	Makes evidence-based decisions.
Havens	Uses positive, healthful-interaction approaches, respecting the integrity of others.
Osler	Lives life in day-tight compartments.
Nightingale, Osler	Extends interests to action at societal policy levels.

remove a thorn from the side of the medical community while, at the same time, helping to correct a societal defect. In this way, Rogers overcame the entrenched, automatic reaction of the medical professions to Federally operated medical services.

These days, too, when it seems incumbent on public figures to build their sense of duty on religious belief and to do so publicly, Paul Rogers is a refreshing phenomenon. Most people do not know what philosophy drives him and cannot guess what his next goal will be as he works to move society forward. He does not wear his personal values on his sleeve.

Rogers is also generous in helping people on a personal level. Because he is America's Mr. Health, it is natural that people ask him, on behalf of themselves or others, for help in finding a good physician or institution, or even for help in addressing a serious nonmedical problem. Rogers is discreet but thorough when getting the right reference. He often makes the first call himself, and checks back to be sure help is forthcoming. If one were to assess Rogers against any set of Machiavellian performance metrics, he would surely fail miserably. Still, it is instructive to apply the metrics of the scholars discussed in chapter 4 to what we know of Rogers' performance (tables 1 and 2). If we agree that Rogers scores high with noted thinkers, with the exception of Machiavelli, on leadership and inner

THE ROGERS MODEL

1. Leadership is educational in nature and personally seen as elevating.
2. Leadership is purposeful and makes things happen.
3. Leadership is a collective activity.
4. Leadership involves positive, healthful interactive approaches at the individual, group, and social levels.
5. Leadership acknowledges that dissension is a fact of life and works to create consensus.
6. Leadership calls for several different leadership styles to be used at different times as appropriate.
7. Leadership creates resonance in others and begets followers.
8. Leadership encompasses self-awareness, self-management, humility, and other-directedness and never veers from the goal.
9. Leadership emanates from a will to move toward a superordinate goal.
10. Leadership reaches beyond the immediate effort to include the larger society.
11. Leadership means always seeking new friends.
12. Leadership includes the capacity to develop and enlarge new consortia and collaborative teams.

strengths, the question arises as to whether Rogers brings anything new to the concept of leadership.

And, indeed, there are at least two such contributions: One is his non-stop interest in making new friends and new contacts. The second is his ability to conceptualize and shape innovative and successful consortia to help him reach his goals. Adding these two traits to a compendium by great thinkers gives us the Rogers Leadership Model.

In addition, his is also a true charismatic personality. That is, his charisma is from the heart. His personal magnetism and persuasiveness spring from a genuine pleasure in being of service to others. Indeed, Rogers' greatest strength as a leader of public citizens lies in the inexorable commitment and performance we see in his 50-year business of improving the health of people.

When this kind of charisma is combined with a powerful intellect and unswerving dedication to the rightness of one's causes, we have a leader capable of bringing society to a higher level of health and better quality of life.

Paul Rogers is clearly a national leader with a broad reach across domestic issues and a genre model for the next generation of great leaders.

Chapter 12

The Rogers Dialogues

In the Fall of 2004, Roger Bulger engaged Paul Rogers in a discussion of health policy over the past half-century, gaining his insight into the leading issues of the day and his best guess about how our society can move to improve the American people's health status.

Q: Mr. Rogers, the following quotation from Lee Atwater, the leading guru of Machiavellian, take-no-prisoners politics in the Reagan and Bush campaigns who died in 1991, is a kind of deathbed recanting of all he had begun in the mid-1980s.

> I was nakedly cruel to Dukakis . . . and I am sorry. My illness [a brain tumor] helped me see what was missing in me. A little heart, a lot of brotherhood (p.31).[1]

If so, it seems to have had little effect on the highly divisive partisan politics that he helped spawn. Do you see any hope now, almost 25 years later, of our leaders reestablishing a civilized leadership in the near future and, if so, how could they achieve that?

A: The heavy division in Congress between the two parties is a serious problem for our nation. It may take some time, but I think the resolution probably must come from the public. Our people may well become frustrated by the results that come from the uncompromising attitudes of so many of today's lawmakers. When the Congress sees that the public is frustrated, it will begin to change. I had hoped that the change would start when the second President Bush came into office. There was some talk about it, but it has not happened. In fact, things may have gotten worse.

All good legislation is basically a compromise. In this way, people who don't agree on every point of a piece of legislation can still get it to a place where it is acceptable to the majority. It may take awhile before the public will fully appreciate that legislation needs to be worked out by both sides.

Q: Educator and civic leader John W. Gardner, while Secretary of Health, Education, and Welfare under President Johnson, implemented Medicare and then, as a private citizen, established Common Cause, a nonpartisan grassroots organization. Gardner holds that leaders must offer moral leadership, articulating goals that lift people out of their "petty silos of self-interest." Did you know Gardner well? Do you agree with his concept of morally purposeful leadership? Whom have you known who meets such a standard?

A: I did know John Gardner, particularly when he was at the Department of Health, Education, and Welfare [now Health and Human Services]. My committee had jurisdiction of that department, so we dealt with John a great deal. I was always impressed with him and his concern with people generally, which exhibited itself in his actions before and after, as well as during, his term as secretary. His work in developing Common Cause grew out of his concern for people, especially those who needed help, who needed some boost. I think he used HEW to push programs that would help people. Some of his actions were definitely in line with that objective.

Q: Most of us can remember the collapse in 1994 of the heralded Clinton plan to provide health insurance for every American. There are those who speculate that both Senator Dole and President Clinton could have joined forces to pass such legislation. One story has it that Clinton rebuffed Dole in such an effort; another has it that Dole couldn't collaborate on it because he would lose conservative support in his run for the Republican Presidential nomination for 1996. Whatever the story actually is, it seems safe to say that party politics kept both men on opposite sides of the fence when in fact both leaders deeply believed in medical coverage for everyone. Isn't this a missed opportunity for collaboration and transformational leadership that could have produced universal coverage years ago?

A: It was a tragedy. Any major national program must have the participation and support of both sides in the Congress and also of the public. Often we find, particularly in the Congress, that people on the hard right and people on the hard left continue to espouse a principle that they would rather talk about endlessly than compromise and get something done! It happens time after time.

Not that either Clinton or Dole were in that position. I like both of them and think they both did a good job generally. However, it was unfortunate that the Clinton plan was drawn up without more input. Some of the people who would be affected, like doctors, were not a part of planning this legislation that would so greatly affect them both in their lives and in the ways that they deal with the public. Also, the timing of the Clinton plan was poor. Clinton made a well-received speech on health insurance. Immediately after, as I recall, he had about an 82 percent rating of approval on his ideas. But it took the White House several months after that speech to send proposed legislation to the Congress. In the interim, the health insurance industry started their ads and, in effect, killed the legislation.

Q: In May 1978, in a speech at the Third Annual Conference on Health Policy, you made the following statements: (1) "The contrast is startling between the runaway spending for healthcare and the resistance of most American business to spending for environmental health protection," and (2) "Most American heavy industry fought every inch of the way against every environmental health requirement with environmental consequences. Every dollar invested to reduce deadly coke oven emissions, to control arsenic and lead from copper smelters, to block unnecessary radiation exposures, to capture chemical plants' carcinogenic discharges, to curb toxic sulfates and nitrate particles from coal combustion, has come only after protracted political and legal struggles."

On October 13, 2004, more than a quarter-century later, you opened a conference at the National Academy of Sciences on Global Environmental Health in the 21st Century: From Governmental Regulation to Corporate Social Responsibility. Laced through the discussions were the following remarks attributed to UN Secretary General Kofi Annan:

1. The private sector cannot prosper if society fails;
2. Government by itself cannot create a successful and sustainable society and world;
3. The world's large multinational corporations have a moral obligation to society to help in its efforts at sustainability; and
4. By extension, all large corporations have a need to define and then fulfill their own corporate societal responsibility.

Do you believe that corporate social responsibility should extend to nongovernmental (i.e., nonprofit) organizations such as universities? To our modern academic health centers and major teaching hospitals?

A: Yes, I think it should, and, indeed, it has. In particular, the academic health centers have assumed a great deal of social responsibility. As I recall, it is their hospitals that provide most of the care for the nation's indigent people.

Large businesses in America have also come a long way in assuming more and more responsibility for helping people in the communities where they are based or conduct business. I believe it is becoming a part of both the American corporate and the nonprofit corporate cultures.

Of course, corporations have to fulfill their responsibilities to the stockholder, but I've seen a lot of change. For instance, several drug companies have led the way to reaching underserved populations abroad by providing medicine for treatment and vaccine for immunization, at times without cost rather than at cost.

All this indicates a developing sense of social responsibility among our corporate and nongovernmental organizations. Given that in 2004 we have some 43 to 45 million people in the United States without health insurance coverage, a number that keeps going up all the time, the Association of Academic Health Centers has started a drive to help get health coverage for everybody. In each state with an academic health center there are now programs to bring the need for universal coverage to the public's attention. This effort is significant, and I think we are beginning to see support for universal health insurance gaining momentum.

Q: The NIH budget has doubled over each fiscal year from 1999 through 2003. Where do we go from here in terms of biomedical research?

A: Well, we have a great deal to do. For example, we still need to see health and health-related programs emphasize the ethics and responsibilities attendant to the delivery of health services, healthcare, and research. We just had some damaging examples of apparent conflicts of interest within the scientific community. One example is the recent revelation of fairly large sums of money that a few scientists, including research lab heads, sometimes get—legally—to consult with specific drug firms; in some instances, they are the makers of drugs being studied at their institute. This freedom to accept honoraria and consultant fees from private interests is the result of good-faith effort by a former NIH director to open up to NIH workers some of the same opportunities available in the world of academe. It has backfired: lack of attention to perceived conflicts of interest was all over the *Washington Post* and *Los Angeles Times* and prompted a full-scale investigation by Congress and an NIH panel. NIH Director Elias Zerhouni has put all such arrangements on hold until a conclusion is reached. The public trust—in fact, my trust—in NIH was diminished significantly by negative reports.*

The Belmont Report of 1979, called for in the National Research Service Award Act that Ted Kennedy and I passed in 1974, was broadly based, but it did lay out the work that needed to be done nationally vis-à-vis ethics and health. One example was the importance of the

* On February 1, 2005, in a dramatic reversal aimed at keeping faith with the public, NIH banned this practice.

institutional review boards in research institutions to make sure that the public is protected and that everything is done right. There is a great deal more to do on this issue, but it is encouraging that we are increasingly conscious of our moral and ethical responsibilities to patients and public alike. Today when problems arise, I think we are very quick to try and correct them.

I believe, too, that under Zerhouni's road map for NIH, basic research will be translated into practice innovation more quickly than before. Here we have a socially responsive and accountable action that will become increasingly apparent to both the public and Congress. NIH is to be commended.

Q: American historian Daniel Boorstin has called America The Republic of Technology. His view is that in our country, the next great technical advance (such as the automobile, steam engine, and telephone in the past, and recently, the Internet) creates in us a vision of seemingly everlasting social progress. In the world of science and healthcare, there is a ring of truth to Boorstin's view. For example, many people are now saying that the electronic medical record's time has come and that its wide dissemination is the crucial next step to achieving a high-quality, cost-effective, and universally available healthcare system for every American. What are your thoughts about this?

A: Well, I believe the electronic medical record is a major advance. Tried in many settings around our country, it has been shown to be effective and must now be made widely available. It is a good next step to increasing the efficiency and the quality of healthcare, especially when it comes to patient safety. The dramatic steps taken by the Veterans Administration to move healthcare quality forward are attributable to its electronic medical-records and bar-coding initiatives in its clinics and hospitals. The future lies in developing successful links between the clinical record and the financial systems, patient-care quality and safety systems, and educational systems that can bring relevant information to clinicians and students in real time. Furthermore, the overall system should provide access to patients so that they can learn more about their ailments and how, in general, to stay well.

The Bush Administration's recent appointment of a national director for information technology in health is an excellent initiative for developing the capacity for interoperability of the evolving medical IT system across the country. It will also be crucial to achieve interoperability between the healthcare and the education pieces.

The National Library of Medicine also has a potentially great role to play in consumer health education. Along with my friend Newt Gingrich, I believe that a growing access to high-quality information is essential for maximizing the health status of our population. The education of the younger generation will inevitably be affected by their experience with getting information on their computer, not to mention their ability to work collaboratively through the Internet rather than face-to-face. This reality, quite well-established at many universities, will find its way into the health-professional curricula, perhaps affecting the classroom and nonclinical elements as well.

Q: It seems that many of our greatest new advances have come upon us suddenly. Magnetic resonance and perhaps even PET scanning technology may be good examples. In contrast, we have the human genome program, a well-planned multiyear Government effort to map the human genome, complete with a set-aside from the beginning to study the ethical implications of potential new tools and interventions. As a result, everyone is far more sophisticated about the matter and better prepared to deal effectively with the fruits of the knowledge flowing from the project. Do you envision any unanticipated discovery that may find us, as a society, unprepared to deal effectively with its implications?

A: The only event that comes to my mind right now is nanotechnology.* It seems that even the scientists at the cutting edge do not know how to communicate with each other; their terminology is still not settled. Nevertheless, they are just rolling along with spectacular scenarios for its use emerging every day. I worry that this technology has the capacity to frighten a wary public, creating a situation where further research is curtailed or even outlawed.

---

* Nanotechnology is the art of manipulating materials on a microscopic or molecular level, for example, creating microscopic robots to aid in the study of cells and microcraft for deep space probes. The device would range from 1 to 100 nanometers across; a nanometer is one-billionth of a meter, or about one ten-thousandth of a human hair.

It is important for academic leaders to start thinking more broadly about the societal implications of this new field and to engage in a continuing dialogue with political and social leaders and the media on the subject. Just look at the total opposition in Europe to genetically altered food products. Yet just the other day, at my local food store, I came upon the grapple, an apple that tastes like a grape! We don't want to mess up legitimate progress in nanotechnology just because we didn't think about ramifications well enough in advance! A process to assure safety must be developed quickly with Government agencies; it is a necessary part of safety assurance.

Q: Throughout your career you have been a strong advocate for a stronger public health system. Since 9/11, you have become more active than ever in building support for a stronger public health infrastructure. What is an adequate national public health infrastructure? And what needs to be done to get from where we are now to where we need to be with all deliberate speed?

A: I think the public health infrastructure is in the process of being reconstructed and getting more support. Of course, a lot of this activity has come out of the 9/11 tragedy, which led us to conclude that many communities all over our nation are not adequately equipped to respond to terrorist attacks. The many efforts already underway to improve competency in handling a terrorist attack make up an important building block in developing adequate public health systems to handle health crises of all kinds, not only terrorist. This situation demands greater attention and more funding, both nationally and at state and local levels.

Q: The shortage of the flu vaccine in 2004 led to long lines of anxious citizens seeking shots before they ran out. As priorities were put in place for children, the elderly, and people with compromised immune systems, no one mentioned rationing. We already ration much of healthcare according to ability to pay. Will there ever be an open discussion of rationing? Does there need to be serious public education regarding the concept of limits? What needs to be done to move from where we are to become a nation providing basic health services to all Americans?

A: Getting healthcare to everyone and health insurance coverage to everyone is a significant undertaking. More then ever, we are finding that gaps in healthcare coverage are growing rather than diminishing. The cost of healthcare delivery is going up. Increases in health insurance rates are now in the double digits, so corporate America is looking for ways to limit the money spent on healthcare benefits. The head of Ford Motor Company recently stated, for example, that Ford will not be able to compete in the global economy if the cost of healthcare benefits continues to rise despite all its best efforts to limit such large increases. It can't compete with auto companies in countries where the government takes care of health insurance. Once industry joins with others in the United States cognizant of the need for healthcare coverage, especially for people who cannot afford healthcare, there may well be some movement.

I think that the position of the National Coalition on Health Care [see chapter 3] will be thrown into the public debate, particularly when the Congress begins to address the problem. It may well take another Presidential election and a series of pre-election debates before people concentrate on healthcare needs. That did not occur in the Bush-Kerry race because most Americans have not felt the economic pinch that seems sure to come with the shifting of healthcare costs to the consumer. If that happens, people will give real thought to universal health coverage, and get really organized to see that it happens. There are many ways that you can cover people: for example, through a tax benefit, beneficiary coverage through the Federal government, or mandated individual coverage. Ultimately, I think that the private sector will be involved and that it will certainly require some increased effort by the Federal and state governments. It goes without saying, of course, that any major program like this has to have bipartisan support.

Q: The increasing trend toward globalization in healthcare; the growing emphasis on prevention of disease; and the "sciences" affecting medical care, public health, and the environment suggest that the United States should become more active in bringing hope to developing countries by sharing more of these resources. If our nation wants to rebuild trust overseas, can healthcare and education become useful tools?

A: I think that a collaborative, international approach at the scientific level can help break through political barriers. We have seen that happen before. When our scientists were working with Soviet scientists during the Cold War, they collaborated with others on programs to better the condition of the world. I think this is true of health programs, too, and the issues associated with global health. We see, both here and abroad, that people in dire need welcome programs to improve health, particularly of children and families. Many Americans and American institutions involved in these kinds of programs report much success, as well as great satisfaction among all those participating and establishing continuing relations.

We really need to concentrate on what can be done in the near future to help improve global health, particularly in areas that are now so alienated from the United States. I think health programs constitute the easiest and best way to begin to build friendships between nations, and perhaps begin to change negative attitudes about us throughout the world. If you come in with health-aid programs not directly governmental and try to educate nationals on improving health status, even training them in their own country, attitudes toward the United States might change. Our schools of public health have done a lot in regard to bringing in nationals from other countries to be trained here so they can return to and improve the health situation in their own countries. That makes friends.

I think it will take governmental support and funding to get adequate and realistic programs going. The sooner we start growing such programs, the better!

Q: Critics of major healthcare reform and universal coverage point out that the USA has quite wonderful population health statistics and that all those people without traditional health insurance or public coverage have access to our hospital emergency rooms and are otherwise taken care of when serious illness or disabling injury afflicts them. In view of these points, why all the fuss about doing better?

A: We have indeed improved our overall mortality data, our life expectancies, and our maternal and infant data, but we are well below the leaders of the world in these categories. Of course, our data are well ahead of data in these categories coming from developing countries. This is because overall American data pools two entirely different cultures, one is the majority group that enjoys good health care and good health and has access to good information and help on health promotion and disease prevention. But the second, though smaller, group, is much closer health-status-wise to the data from a developing country than to that from the majority of Americans. Thus, we have marked disparities in health, life expectancy, maternal, and infant mortality among significant subgroups.* Since we know for a fact that having health insurance correlates well with improving health status, there are no logical grounds for not working to fix these inequities and inequalities of opportunity among our citizens. Without adequate health coverage, there are too many cases where people defer important drugs or other interventions so they can cover rent and food for their families; then they end up either losing their life or suffering a catastrophic illness. These problems are concentrated not among those with no jobs, but rather among the so-called working poor, the very people trying hardest to get out of the poverty cycle.

Q: If you were by some magical force returned right now to the leadership position of your old subcommittee in the House of Representatives, do you think you would be able to accomplish as much as you did in the 1970s?

A: Well, that would be mighty hard to do, mostly because of the sharply polarized political environment. It's not that it was always easy to get bipartisan support on a project, but it was nowhere near as difficult and challenging as it is these days. In the old days, we were able to be much more inclusive of everyone, and the minority members were always present and accounted for in all hearings relevant to important legislation. Our openness to dissenting views and our ability to include some other people's ideas in the

* In 2000, infant mortality in the United States was down to 6.9 deaths per 1,000 births, and maternal mortality had decreased to 11.8 deaths per 100,000 live births. There are significant differences in these rates between whites and minorities. Black infants, for example, are more than twice as likely to die than white infants, and black mothers are over three times as likely to die—and these disparities are increasing. Life span overall was 77.2 years, with black women expected to live 5.1 fewer years and black men 6.6 fewer years than their white counterparts.[2]

final bill created an atmosphere of mutual support when crunch time inevitably came.

One could go on and on about the good old days, but I don't believe the current environment will give way to something more collaborative and friendly until the voters insist on that from the people they elect. We have a long way to go to achieve that goal, but today is the first day of the rest of our lives and would be a good day to start work on that.

Q: You have enlisted an extraordinary number of people from a dazzling array of walks of life in various policy efforts. Many of them have since become much more visible public leaders in different advocacy causes, bearing ample testimony to your success as a transformational leader. Since we can agree that most of your missions are still works in progress, doesn't it follow that there must be an ongoing effort to recruit more leaders to continue such efforts? How should we go about finding them?

A: This is true, and much is being done to involve as many people as possible in health leadership roles. But it still is not at an appropriate level for establishing these health concerns in the minds of others. Yet the need is so great, and some ways to fill that need so apparent. We have the American International Health Alliance and Project Hope, for instance, working to establish partnerships between the United States and other nations. I know that many health professionals use their summer vacation to go abroad to provide healthcare services. We need more scientists, doctors, dentists, nurses, pharmacists, and public health professionals consciously spreading the great knowledge that we have developed in the health field. We need more people to speak up and make our own people appreciate how vital such programs are to our nation's well-being. We very much need the friendship of other nations in this day and age.

Q: Was it always your ambition to become the go-to guy in health policy? Or did you seek to become the most effective public servant and citizen-advocate for health you could be? If the latter is the case, was it serendipity that got you into health, science, and the environment?

A: As a young lawyer in West Palm Beach, I worked with the local heart and cancer associations. This gave me some exposure to some of the problems they work to solve. Dad's sudden death from a heart attack made me even more conscious of health issues. When I came to Congress, one of the people who helped me develop a better understanding of the importance of health matters was the chair of the Interstate and Foreign Commerce Committee, Oren Harris, the Democratic congressman from Arkansas. Well before my seniority on the committee warranted it, he made me chairman of an ad hoc committee to do oversight on the National Institutes of Health. I came to understand how that organization operated and worked, and I found it fascinating. I came to know and believe, very strongly, that without research there is no hope for prevention, diagnosis, treatment, or cure of the diseases that affect the citizens of this nation.

Q: Many of your friends and colleagues express awe at your staying power and continuing enthusiasm for the causes you hold so dear: public health, environmental health, and health research. In many people, such dedication arises from a belief system based upon the greater good. No one knows your religion or if you practice any religion at all. With the understanding that religious belief is fundamentally a highly personal matter, would you care to comment on whether any of it plays a role in your sense of direction?

A: I am a little surprised that people can't figure out whether or not I am religious. Becky and I don't like to talk about it that much, partly because it may tend to separate us from people with different beliefs, and partly because it does seem to be a private matter. But I will tell you that I am religious. I have ended every day, for as long as I remember—up to and including last night—by getting down on my knees by my bed to say my prayers, just like my father did every day of his life!

Appendix A

Selected Health Legislation Passed Under the Leadership of Paul Rogers, 1962-78

1962

Migrant Health Act (P.L. 87-692)

Authorized grants to community nonprofit organizations for a broad array of medical and support services to migrant and seasonal farm workers and their families.

1963

Mental Retardation Facilities and Community Mental Health Centers Construction Act (P.L. 88-164)

Established a Federal grant program to create community mental health centers that provided inpatient, outpatient, and partial hospitalization for persons with mental illness and construct facilities for people with mental retardation, with a special focus on those who would fare better by living within the community.

1968

Radiation Control for Health and Safety Act (P.L. 90-602)

Provided for the protection of the public health and safety from the dangers of electronic product radiation by setting manufacturing standards and giving the Federal government the authority to inspect the facilities of manufacturers under certain circumstances.

continued

1970

Comprehensive Drug Abuse Prevention and Control Act (P.L. 91-513)

Brought increased national efforts to drug abuse prevention, rehabilitation, and treatment programs. Replaced the Narcotic Addict Rehabilitation Act's definition of "narcotic addict" with "drug-dependent person," making it possible to extend Federal rehabilitation and treatment programs to non-opiate abusers. It also established the Commission on Marijuana and Drug Abuse on which Paul Rogers served as a member.

Clean Air Act (P.L. 91-604)

Required the EPA to establish national ambient air-quality standards and required automobile manufacturers to reduce emissions by 90 percent between model year 1970 and model year 1975.

Emergency Health Personnel Act (P.L. 91-623)

Established the National Health Services Corps Program in an effort to eliminate shortages of health professionals in medically underserved communities. It also authorized government loans for costs of tuition and other educational expenses incurred by health professionals, with repayment in exchange for providing primary health services in these communities.

1971

Health Professionals Education Assistance Act (P.L. 92-157)

Established an innovative program of capitation grants to medical schools and other schools of the health professions, based on student enrollment, in return for promised increases in class size. It also established several special-project grant programs that enhanced Federal support for family medicine departments and fellowships at area health education centers where health professions students are trained in sites remote from medical centers; for physician-assistant training; and for other programs deemed to be of national priority.

Nurse Training Act (P.L. 92-158)

Addressed the need for training and retaining nurses through capitation grants to nursing schools as well as through loans, loan forgiveness, and scholarships for nursing students. This law also promoted training of nurse practitioners in baccalaureate programs, contributing to national efforts to give nurses increased responsibilities in caring for patients.

National Cancer Act (P.L. 92-218)

Established a National Cancer Program to coordinate Federal cancer research initiatives at NCI as well as a National Cancer Advisory Board to evaluate the national cancer program. It also established authority for national comprehensive cancer centers and cancer control programs.

1972

Drug Abuse Office and Treatment Act (P.L. 92-255)

Established a Special Action Office for Drug Abuse Treatment and Prevention within the White House to coordinate the nation's drug abuse efforts, after congressional hearings revealed the fragmented nature of Federal efforts to combat drug trafficking and provide treatment for drug addicts and abusers.

National Sickle Cell Anemia Control Act (P.L. 92-294)

Increased attention to, and Federal funding of, research on, and screening programs for Sickle Cell Anemia, which affects African Americans.

Drug Listing Act (P.L. 92-387)

Provided FDA with information on what drugs were on the market by requiring manufacturers to register drugs and their ingredients as well as to submit copies of their labeling and advertising. The Kefauver-Harris Amendments of 1962 had required that all pharmaceutical products marketed after 1938 be shown to be effective (as well as safe).

National Heart, Blood Vessel, Lung, and Blood Act (P.L. 92-423)

Upgraded the National Heart, Blood, and Lung Institute, based largely on the 1971 legislation upgrading the status of the National Cancer Institute, by enhancing its authority to provide for expanded, intensified, and coordinated activities in heart and lung disease research and training.

continued

Communicable Disease Control Amendments (P.L. 92-449)

Provided direction and funding to the CDC for the control and prevention of communicable diseases through immunization and other preventative programs.

National Cooley's Anemia Control Act (P.L. 92-414)

Established a national program for treatment of and research into Cooley's anemia (thalassemia) which occurs primarily among persons of Mediterranean, African, or Southeastern Asian descent.

National Advisory Commission on Multiple Sclerosis Act (P.L. 92-563)

Established a national advisory commission to determine the most effective means of finding the cause of, and cure and treatments for, multiple sclerosis.

Noise Control Act (P.L. 92-574)

Required the Federal government to establish and enforce uniform noise-control standards for aircraft.

Emergency Health Personnel Act Amendments (P.L. 92-585)

Continued and improved the National Health Service Corps Program, under which physicians agreed to practice in medically underserved areas across the country in return for scholarships and loan forgiveness.

1973

Emergency Medical Services Act (P.L. 93-154)

Provided communities with Federal assistance for developing comprehensive area emergency medical service systems. It was based on experience in Vietnam that demonstrated that more immediate access to healthcare could save countless lives.

Health Maintenance Organization Act (P.L. 93-222)

Provided Federal support—loans, loan guarantees, and grants— to encourage the establishment of health maintenance organizations that would meet specific statutory requirements.

1974

Sudden Infant Death Syndrome Act (P.L. 93-270)

Provided Federal assistance for providing information and education on SIDS.

Narcotic Addict Treatment Act (P.L. 93-281)

Amended the Controlled Substances Act to give HEW (now HHS) authority to establish treatment standards and gave the attorney general the authority to establish security standards for practitioners who treat narcotic drug abusers. It also required registration of practitioners with the attorney general.

Comprehensive Alcohol Abuse and Alcoholism Prevention, Treatment, and Rehabilitation Act (P.L. 93-282)

Extended and improved Federal alcoholism grant and contract authorities to combat and treat alcoholism, recently classified as a disease by the American Medical Association. Perhaps its most important feature was authority for HEW to award special grants to states that had enacted a model state law that approached alcoholism from a health standpoint.

Research on Aging Act (P.L. 93-296)

Established the National Institute on Aging within NIH, with responsibility to conduct research related to diseases and other special health problems for the aged.

National Research Service Award Act (P.L. 93-348)

Responded to a decision by the Nixon Administration to terminate long-standing postdoctoral research and education programs at NIH by continuing and enhancing a national program of biomedical research fellowships, traineeships, and training to assure the continued excellence of biomedical research in the United States.

continued

National Diabetes Mellitus Research and Education Act (P.L. 93-354)

Required more effective efforts in research and public education on diabetes after evidence that a national program to coordinate and enhance the NIH programs against diabetes mellitus was needed.

Safe Drinking Water Act (P.L. 93-523)

Established a new environmental program, administered by the EPA, requiring that water supply systems meet minimum national standards for protection of public health. It was based on findings that the nation's public water systems were polluted.

1975

National Arthritis Act (P.L. 93-640)

Expanded legislative programs to focus on specific diseases by requiring the NIAMDD to implement a national attack on arthritis.

National Health Planning and Resources Development Act (P.L. 93-641)

Required the development of a national health policy, of state and area health-planning and resources programs, and of regional health-systems agencies responsible for establishing and implementing health-systems plans designed to ensure more rational delivery of healthcare. This law was one of the most important Federal efforts to control healthcare costs.

Public Health Service Act Amendments (P.L. 94-63)

Extended and expanded some of the most significant Federal health programs of the 1960s to respond to national public health needs. It also revised and extended programs for Federal support of state comprehensive health services, family planning programs, and community mental health centers.

Developmentally Disabled Assistance and Bill of Rights Act (P.L. 94-103)

Made substantial revisions in the Federal program of support to university-affiliated facilities and to states to assist in delivery of services to persons with developmental disabilities, and established their statutory rights to treatment, services, and habilitation, thereby making significant improvements in earlier Federal health legislation on this matter.

1976

Amendments to Drug Abuse Office and Treatment Act (P.L. 94-237)

Required that hospitals receiving Federal assistance not discriminate against drug abusers or people addicted to drugs in admission or treatment. The legislation was in response to some hospitals' refusal to provide agency care.

National Sickle Cell Anemia, Cooley's Anemia, Tay-Sachs, and Genetic Diseases Act (P.L. 94-278)

Combined and expanded the National Sickle Cell Anemia Control Act of 1972 and the National Cooley's Anemia Control Act of 1972, to cover funding of research for a wide variety of genetic diseases.

Medical Device Amendments (P.L. 94-295)

Amended the Food, Drug, and Cosmetic Act to assure the safety and effectiveness of medical devices by establishing a classification system for devices and requiring that their regulation be determined by classification. Before this, the FDA's authority over medical devices was minimal, with the agency forced to treat some medical devices as drugs so that premarket approval could be based on clinical trials.

National Consumer Health Information and Health Promotion Act (P.L. 94-317)

Responded to the public's interest in gaining information relevant to disease prevention and good health practices. The law required formulation of national goals and strategies for health-information and health-promotion activities, preventative health services, and education in the appropriate use of healthcare; and authorized support of research, community programs and information. It also authorized grants to states and public nonprofit entities to assist them in meeting costs of disease prevention and

continued

control programs, including emphasis on extending immunization programs and programs to combat venereal disease.

National Swine Flu Immunization Program Act (P.L. 94-380)

Authorized grants and contracts to immediately mount a national swine flu vaccination program and protected organizations, individuals, and manufacturers against liability for injuries arising from administration of the vaccine other than those occurring as a result of negligence.

Indian Health Care Improvement Act (P.L. 94-437)

Established Federal responsibility for the healthcare and education of American Indians by improving the services and facilities of Federal Indian health programs.

Health Professions Educational Assistance Act (P.L. 94-484)

Continued, with substantial modification, the programs of assistance to health-professions schools and students and the National Health Service Corps program, thereby reintensifying efforts to increase the percentage of primary healthcare teaching programs and to support efforts against geographic misdistribution of healthcare professionals.

1977

Amendments to the Clean Air Act of 1970 (P.L. 95-95)

Required all power plants, no matter their age and size, to install the best antipollution technology. These amendments also set new auto-emissions standards.

Medicare–Medicaid Anti-Fraud and Abuse Amendments (P.L. 95-142)

Strengthened the capability of the Federal government to detect, prosecute, and punish fraudulent activities under the Medicare and Medicaid programs.

Rural Health Clinics (P.L. 95-210)

Amended the Medicare and Medicaid laws to provide for separate payments for rural health clinic services in addition to those being provided for hospital and physician services.

1978

Psychotropic Substances Act (P.L. 95-633)

Amended the Comprehensive Prevention and Control Act to meet obligations under the Convention on Psychotropic Substances relating to regulatory controls on the manufacture, distribution, importation, and exportation of psychotropic substances.

Rehabilitation, Comprehensive Services, and Developmental Disabilities Amendments (P.L. 95-602)

Increased Federal responsibilities substantially to assure appropriate opportunities for people with disabilities. It established community service employment programs, programs for independent living, and other specialized programs for people with disabilities, and also established a National Institute on Handicapped Research within HEW.

Health Services Research, Health Statistics, and Health Care Technology Act (P.L. 95-623)

Established a National Center for Health Care Technology within HEW and required the Institute of Medicine to conduct a study of the health costs of pollution and other environmental condition. It was enacted on the final day of Rogers' congressional career.

Appendix B

Organizational Affiliations, Honorary Degrees, and Awards, Paul Rogers, 2004

ORGANIZATIONAL AFFILIATIONS

American Cancer Society

American Federation for Aging Research

Campaign for Medical Research

Campaign for Public Health

Foundation for Biomedical Research

Friends of the National Library of Medicine

Global Health Council

Harvard School of Public Health Dean's Council

National Academy of Sciences Institute of Medicine Roundtable on Environmental Health, Sciences, Research, and Medicine

National Council on Patient Information and Education

National Foundation for Infectious Diseases

National Osteoporosis Foundation

Research!America

HONORARY DEGREES

Albany Medical College of Union University, Doctor of Science

Commonwealth University of Virginia, Doctor of Science

Duke University, Doctor of Laws

Florida Atlantic University, Doctor of Laws

Georgetown University, Doctor of Laws

George Washington University, Doctor of Laws

Hahnemann Medical College, Doctor of Humane Letters

Long Island University, Doctor of Laws

Medical University of South Carolina, Doctor of Medical Science

New York College of Podiatric Medicine, Doctor of Humane Letters

New York Medical College, Doctor of Humane Letters

Nova University, Doctor of Humanities

University of Florida, Doctor of Laws

University of Maryland, Doctor of Laws

University of Miami, Doctor of Science

AWARDS

1978 Dedication of the Paul G. Rogers Federal Building and Courthouse, West Palm Beach, Florida

1982 Public Welfare Medal, National Academy of Sciences

1991 Health Policy Award, National Health Lawyers Association
Year 2000 Award, National Cancer Institute

1993 Albert Lasker Award for Public Service, Lasker Foundation

1994 Hugo H. Schaefer Award, American Pharmaceutical Association

Award in Aging, AlliedSignal Achievement

Distinguished Leadership Award, University of Florida Health Sciences Center

continued

1995 Leadership Award, National Osteoporosis Foundation

1996 Maxwell Finland Award for Scientific Achievement, National Foundation for Infectious Diseases

1997 Distinguished Service Award, American Cancer Society

1998 Distinguished Americans Award, National Community Pharmacists Association

1999 Outstanding Citizen Award, IONA Senior Services

Golden Eagle Award, National Association of Physicians for the Environment

Paul G. Rogers Award (first recipient), Association of Academic Health Centers

2000 Dedication of main plaza at the National Institutes of Health as the Paul G. Rogers Plaza by an Act of Congress 2001

Medal of Honor for Cancer Control, American Cancer Society

Adam Yarmolinsky Medal, National Institute of Medicine

2004 Distinguished Service Award, National Library of Medicine Board of Regents

Endnotes

ENDNOTES

Introduction

1. Statistical Abstract of the United States, Compiled by Edward Whitney (Washington: Government Printing Office, 1922) p. 54.

2. Grove, Robert D., and Alice M. Hetzel, Vital Statistics Rates in the United States, 1940-1960 (Washington: U.S. Department of Health, Education, and Welfare, Public Health Service, 1968) p. 309.

3. Linder, Forrest S., and Robert D. Grove, Vital Statistics Rates in the United States, 1900-1940 (Washington: U.S, Department of Health, Education, and Welfare, Public Health Service, 1947) p. 620.

4. Ibid, p. 572.

5. Grove, Robert D., and Alice M. Hetzel, Vital Statistics Rates in the United States, 1940-1960 (Washington: U.S. Department of Health, Education, and Welfare, Public Health Service, 1968) p. 309.

6. Ibid. p. 296.

7. Ibid. p. 214.

Chapter 3

1. Eilperin, Juliet, U.S. Faces 'Pivotal Moment' on Clean Air Regulation. Washington Post, 27 January 2005.

Chapter 7

1. Anylan, William G., Metamorphosis: Memoirs of a Life in Medicine (North Carolina: Duke University Press, 2004).

Chapter 10

1. Burns, James MacGregor, Leadership (New York: Harper & Row, 1978).

2. Wright, Robert, What Would Machiavelli Do? The New York Times, 2 August 2004.

3. Phillips, Robert, American Dynasty: Aristocracy, Fortune, and the Politics of Deceit in the House of Bush (New York: Viking, 2004).

4. Goleman, Daniel, Emotional Intelligence: Why It Can Matter More Than IQ (New York: Bantam Books, 1995).

5. Goleman, Daniel, Richard Boyatzis, and Annie McKee, Primal Leadership: Learning to Lead with Emotional Intelligence (Boston: Harvard Business School Press, 2002).

6. Collins, James, Good to Great: Why Some Companies Make the Leap and Others Do Not (New York: HarperBusiness, 2001).

7. Collins, Jim. Built to Last: Successful Habits of Visionary Companies (New York: HarperBusiness, 1994).

8. Modified from the table in Collins, Good to Great, p. 20.

9. Frankl, Viktor E., Man's Search for Meaning, trans. Illse Lasche (Boston: Beacon Press, 1962).

10. Havens, Leston L., Making Contact: Uses of Language in Psychotherapy (Cambridge: Harvard University Press, 1986).

11. Hamer, Dean, The God Gene: How Faith Is Hardwired Into Our Genes (New York: Random House, 2004).

12. Engel, George, The Need for a New Medical Model: A Challenge for Biomedicine, Science 196(1977):129–136.

13. Osler, Sir William, A Way of Life: An Address to Yale Students (Baltimore, Remington Putnam Book Company, 1932).

14. Osler, Sir William, Aequanimitas: With Other Addresses to Medical Students, Nurses and Practitioners of Medicine (London: H. K. Lewis, 1904).

15. Osler, William, Man's Redemption of Man. A Lay Sermon. Delivered at McEwan Hall, Edinburgh, Sunday, July 2, 1910. Published with preface and annotations by Lawrence Longo on the occasion of the Joint Meeting of the American Osler Society, the Osler Club of London, the Japan Osler Society, and the Scottish Society of the History of Medicine Edinburgh, Scotland, Sunday, July 2, 1910 (Loma Linda, California: Loma Linda University Press, 2004).

16. For an in-depth review of Nightingale's life and work, see the following: Gillian Gill, The Extraordinary Life of Miss Florence (New York: Random House Publishing Group, 2004); Rob van der Peet, The Nightingale Model of Nursing: An Analysis Of Florence Nightingale's Concepts of Nursing, and Their Impact On Present Day Practice (Edinburgh: Campion Press, 1995); Florence Nightingale, Notes on Nursing; What It Is and What It Is Not (New York: Dover Publications, 1969); and Michael Calabria and Janet Macrae, eds. Florence Nightingale Suggestions for Thought: Selections and Commentaries (Philadelphia: University of Pennsylvania Press, 1994).

Chapter 12

1. Quoted by David Orr, Professor of Environmental Studies, Oberlin University, The Last Refuge—Patriotism, Politics and the Environment in an Age of Terror (Island Press, Washington and London, 2004).

2. The 20th Century Legacy: Drops in Infant and Maternal Mortality, Women's Health in Primary Care, 3:1 (January 2000); National Vital Statistics Reports, U.S. Life Tables December 2004 (Washington: National Center for Health Statistics) in press.

About the Authors

ROGER J. BULGER brings to this work his distinguished 30-year background in healthcare leadership. Currently president of the Association of Academic Health Centers, he was previously president of the University of Texas Health Sciences Center at Houston and chancellor of the University Massachusetts Medical Center at Worcester, as well as dean of the medical school. He also was the first executive officer of the Institute of Medicine, National Academy of Sciences.

Dr. Bulger has held tenured academic posts in internal medicine, community medicine, and public health at four major universities, concentrating his clinical and laboratory research in infectious diseases and the clinical pharmacology of antibiotics. He holds numerous awards for his work; served on various professional, corporate, and nonprofit boards in the healthcare and health sciences fields; and is the author of many works dealing with the healthcare arena. He lives with his wife in Washington, D.C. They have two grown daughters.

SHIRLEY SIROTA ROSENBERG has been a writer, editor, and journalist for all her professional life (even in college), and taught what it is she does in the Publications Specialist Program, George Washington University. As Washington correspondent for *Parents' Magazine*, she covered the healthcare-research beat when she was raising her children, and has worked with Dr. Bulger and his staff at the Association of Academic Health Centers on many publications. Over a 40-year career, Rosenberg has also written for many national magazines and served as lead editor on numerous high-level government publications. Rosenberg lives in Washington, D.C., with her husband. They have a grown son and daughter.

Other Publications by the Authors

Roger J. Bulger

Hippocrates Revisited
In Search of the Modern Hippocrates
Medical Professional Liability and the Delivery of Obstetrical Care—
An Interdisciplinary Review
Mission Management: A New Synthesis
Physician and Philosopher: The Philosophical Foundation of Medicine, Essays by Dr. Edmund Pellegrino
The Quest for Mercy
Technology, Bureaucracy and Healing in America: A Post-modern Paradigm

Shirley Sirota Rosenberg

Writer
American Red Cross Family Health Series
The First Oil Rush
How Children Grow
Staying Connected: A Guide to Raising a Teenage Daughter

Lead Editor
The First Special Report on Alcohol and Health
Forging Partnerships for Africa's Future
The Forgiveness Factor
Gender-Based Violence: Emerging Issues in Programs Serving Displaced Populations
Mud, Muscle, and Miracles